A-A-AMERICA!
& STONE

A-A-America! is a double-bill consisting of *Grandma Faust*, a burlesque, and *The Swing*, a documentary. It was written for Inter-Action's 'American Connection' season and first staged at the Almost Free Theatre, London, in 1976.

The short play, *Stone*, was written for Gay Sweatshop and first performed at the ICA Theatre, London, the same year.

For this edition the author has revised all three plays and provided new introductory notes to both parts of **A-A-America!**

In his Note to *Stone*, Bond writes about injustice. Wh⸳ applies equally to all three plays in this vol⸳ 'To support an injustice to anyor⸳ involves you in physical repressi⸳ extreme cases cost you your life. and emotional distortions. To jus⸳ with myths — for example, that p⸳ bad, the tory party is made up of ⸳ smash the country. This distortion ⸳⸳⸳uman relationships; and, as it prevents the rational solution of problems, it produces hysteria and violence. Ultimately all major repressions — Nazi anti-semitism, black slavery, the persecution of homosexuals — are signs of the injustice of a whole society.'

Edward Bond

A-A-AMERICA!
&
STONE

EYRE METHUEN · LONDON

First published in Great Britain in 1976 in the Methuen New
Theatrescripts series by Eyre Methuen Ltd., 11 New Fetter Lane,
London, EC4P 4EE. Re-issued in Methuen Modern Plays
in this re-set and revised edition in 1981, Copyright © 1976,
1981 by Edward Bond 'The Little Grey Bonnet' copyright ©
1911 by Chappell & Co. Ltd. Reproduced by kind permission.
Words and music by Lionel Monckton.
Set in IBM 10pt Journal by 🅣 Tek-Art, Croydon, Surrey.
Printed by Whitstable Litho Ltd., Whitstable, Kent

ISBN 0 413 48320 7

Grandma Faust

A burlesque

The first part of A-A-AMERICA!

Author's Note

This isn't a buffoon play. The characters shouldn't be 'sent up'
by the players. It should be played almost as if it were restoration
comedy. The matter of the play is highly emotional. This will
inevitably come through, but the players should not seek it.
Instead, they must play the wit, clarity and precision of their
lines and actions — seeking for neither anger nor laughter.

The play isn't about the struggle for black power. It's about the
cruelty and depravity of those whites who persecute blacks.
Nevertheless it was necessary to show a black response in order
to describe the world of the whites. But I didn't want to show
the tactics of the fight for black freedom. Instead it was enough
(in this play) to show the persistence of Paul's integrity and his
developing understanding of his situation. He mustn't be acted
either as cunning or as simply and naively good. He is rather
serious. He moves from famine and slavery to prosperity and
freedom because he is not corrupted by the whites (and turned
into an 'inner white man') but instead learns who both he and
they are, and in doing so learns that he is strong enough to make
his own victory certain. That is all this play needs to show about
Paul. He appears later in *The Swing*. If both plays are played
together Paul must be played by the same actor.

Grandma Faust was first presented by the Ambiance Lunch-Hour Theatre Club at Inter-Action's Almost Free Theatre, London, on 25 October 1976. The cast was as follows:

UNCLE SAM	Chris Malcolm
GRANDMA FAUST	Henry Woolf
PAUL	Don Warrington
LADY 1	Geraldine James
LADY 2	Glen Walford
ASSISTANT 1	Ron Travis
ASSISTANT 2	Garry Whelan

Directed by Jack Emery
Designed by Norman Coates
Lighting by Suresa Galbraith
Sound by Pete Mount
Wardrobe by Monica Strauss

The setting should be simple.

Scene One

River bank.

UNCLE SAM *stands fishing in the river.*

SAM. There's all those little silver fish down there aglintin like
the sun in the lawd's blue eyes. Those little silver fish are so
purty if I ever catched them I could buy the whole world.
Every river an mountain an the fields an seas. But not one of
those little critters jumps on the end of my little tin hook.
Hot diggety.

GRAN (*brings herself in, in a wheelchair. She is a cross between
Whistler's Mother and Grandma Moses*). Howdee son.

SAM. Howdee gran.

GRAN. What you catched today?

SAM. Shucks gran. No need t' beat about the bush as the lawd
said t' Moses when he set fire t' the Chuckahoney Tree. Ain
catched nothin.

GRAN. What bait you usin boy?

SAM. Nothin.

GRAN. Holdee boy. You mean t' tell me you're astood standin
there with your line adanglin in the water — which is sure
gonna give simple-minded folks like your grandma here the
idea you're fishin — an you *aint?*

SAM (*scratches his head*). Well . . . I'm *tryin* t' fish.

GRAN. This won't do at all son. You tell your grandma the
meanin of this here. Come on now boy.

SAM. Shucks gran times is so bad I just can't afford bait.

GRAN. You gotta give your fish somethin t' eat afore you can
catch em. That's the way of the world as writ down in the
good book. Cast your bread upon the waters.

SAM. Ain got no bread.

GRAN. This is a squanderous age. They devour their seed corn and
and wander in the desert.

SAM *throws his rod on the ground.*

SAM. Shucks gran I've been meaning t' say this since I was knee-high to a rattle snake. You dont-ought-a-shouldnt keep quoting the good book at folks. Sounds as if you were trying t' put the lawd down. You know something gran? You can make the word of the lawd sound real mean. No disrespect to any creature great or small. But that's how it is. Hot diggety.

GRAN. I can see you're most irrascitated son. Well the time has come for a little close-circuit inter-family chat-show. I have somethin t' confess son.

SAM. Shucks ain no call t' over do it gran, every folks round here knows tell of your indiscretion with Captain James FitzClarence back in the old days. I guess the captain was a gentlemen or you wouldnt have had nothing t' —

GRAN. O I was a real fire-ball in silk satin when I was a gall. But this ain about no Captain FitzClarence. It's this son: your gran is the devil.

SAM. Shucks gran you ain that bad.

GRAN. It's the lawd's honest truth I'm tellin you.

SAM. You're a bit mean — folks ain never gonna fall out over that! An you git some real bad days. But you ain no devil gran.

GRAN. I'm tellin you the truth boy. I ain sayin no figurative fancy talk. I am the devil out the smokey pit.

SAM. You don't look like the devil goddam it. Good an ugly, sure. But I thought the devil had horns an a tail — an breathed real *hot* fire, not jist the ol' cross-patch talk you holla out sometimes —

GRAN. If'n I went round dress-up like that I'd git nowhere. The bad folks 'd scoot-an-scaddle like an unbroke pony with a hairy cannon ball up his hoof — an the bold folks 'd just laugh.

SAM. Let em laugh. You're the devil? —you jist pick em up the end of your pitch fork an toss em in the smokey pit.

GRAN. Ain s'easy as that. You have t' use temptation, git em so darn horny *they* run after *you*. I ain the lawd round here, I'm just the servant.

SAM. Can't follow that. Left school the day I learned how t' climb an apple tree and I ain goin back now. Why you tellin me all this for gran?

GRAN. If things as bad as you says then I'm gonna intervene.

SAM. If you're the devil you jist git those little silver fish t' hop on the end of my hook. Don't sit there on your ass sassin like some little ol' school lady.

GRAN. You treat me respectable boy. I may be the devil but I'm likewise your gran — an on one of those scores I deserves respect. I can't jist put the fish on your hook boy. The devil ain allowd t' do no good turns. Sometimes I have t' act so devious I confuse myself. Now I'll tell you what I'll do. What day is t'morra?

SAM. Today is June eighth. So sure as ever t'morra's June — er — (*Counts on his fingers.*) Know'd I should have stayed in school for one more lesson.

GRAN. You're gettin there boy.

SAM. June ninth! Great Nigger Foot Pie Day!

GRAN. That's it son (*Sentimentally:*) Nigger Foot Pie Day.

SAM. Well it ain gonna be so celebratory for me none! Can't afford a fish lunch let alone no Nigger Foot Pie. T'morra is gonna be the worst most miserablest Nigger Foot Pie Day I ever had. Think I'll spend the day in bed. Don't wanna hear all that jubilation crunchin of teeth an smackin of lips an smell that ol' smoked-nigger aromee in the air — when I can't afford my own pie. I ain havin the left-overs from next-door's pie. Go without nothin sooner'n have my pie served up with charity sauce an humility beer.

GRAN. Now son —

SAM. Hangdog gran if'n you're the devil you ought-a-gotta have a little understandin of a man's pride.

GRAN. Don't you give me no theological back-chat son. Pride's a cup of cold water served in a mug of gold. But you can't even afford water!

SAM. Shucks-hangdog-diggey-de!

GRAN. Now I can give you all the Nigger Foot Pies you ever could eat. An nigger roast an fricassee of nigger —

SAM. Now gran you'll have my mouth awaterin so much this here river's gonna overflow.

GRAN. Spare nigger fingers with coleslaw as side dish. Nigger fat soup.

SAM. YOW-EEEE!

GRAN. An nigger elbows to take away from table afterwards an pick by the fire.

SAM. *Huh-huh!*

GRAN. An all the river an valleys an mountains of this world. Cause I'm gonna make them little silver fish jump like grass-hoppers right on the end of your hook. An then you can afford most everythin else.

SAM. You sure are the devil. Can't say I ain had my suspicions in the past. Now if you're offerin me all the fruits an goodies of this world, you're after one thing. (*Taps his chest.*) What the Reverend Hosia Williams call my silent ticker. You gotta offer more gran.

GRAN (*nods and smiles*). Go on son.

SAM. My soul's got muscle. I want the whole wide world. I want the moon, both sides. I want the stars — and the territory in between.

GRAN (*nodding and grinning*). An Nigger Foot Pie like mother made it.

SAM. Shucks gran you ate one Nigger Foot Pie you ate em all. Most every.

GRAN. Son I can see that! Ain hardly decent that boney ol' chin with hairy grey stubble stickin through adribblin an aspittlin like a babe. Well that don't shock me none. I understand temptation. Son if you was t' offer me your soul done up in purty paper an fancy ribbons for christmas — I'd jist have t' act contrary t' all the customs of that season of goodwill and decline — decline — your offer.

SAM. Holdee. Is that some sort of insult?

GRAN (*shrugs*). Don't intend no insult boy. But you been playin ducks an drakes with your soul so long it's mortgaged out most-place-everywhere an I could foreclose on that article anytime without you even knowin. You gotta *own* your soul before you can sell it.

SAM (*righteous*). Ain quarrellin on the eve of Nigger Foot Pie

Day.

GRAN. Git your hands on those fish an every day's gonna be Nigger Foot Pie Day.

SAM. Glory be my stomach's rumblin like the ghosts of them dead bisons runnin on the great plain. What do I have t' do?

GRAN. Nothin. Almost. Won't trouble you any. But it'll satisfy your ol' gran.

SAM. Well what?

GRAN. I want you — (*She interrupts herself.*) An see-here boy I'll be right behind you, you'll have all the help I've got, I'll draw up the deed an you sign the bottom, why I'll even draw a dotted line for —

SAM. Gran you're a wicked sly ol' tease. Now you stop hangin about like that an tell what you're cookin up for Nigger Foot Pie Day.

GRAN. I declare, that boy's making devil's jokes now! Look how your ol' chin's awobblin an adribblin. You're so atremble your soul's gonna pop out with fright an go fly away over that river.

SAM. I ain atremble nothin. I can see you're in a real good mood gran, so there's nothin t' worry about. I'm agrinnin count of I'm watchin the sauciest ol' shrewdest pole-cat that ever tried t' claw the eyes out her own shadow.

GRAN. Well thank you son. Now I'll tell you. Jist sell me the soul of another man.

SAM. What man?

GRAN. No one you know.

SAM (*relief*). Hangdog for a moment I thought I had t' retail the soul of the Reverend Hosia Williams.

GRAN (*chuckles with delight*). Why bless your precious body I had ol' Hosia's soul long ago.

SAM (*sudden idea*). Now gran you ain up t' no real bad tricks? I ain gotta sell the soul of Mr President?

GRAN (*laughs with delight*). Dear, dear. (*Dabs her eyes.*) Dear, dear. (*Shakes her head and smiles.*) That boy'll be the death of me. (*Bursts into laughter again.*) Dear dear. Tch tch tch . . .

(*Composes herself. To* SAM:) I ain after — (*Bursts into laughter again.*) Dear dear. My my my. (*Calms herself.*) I ain after no Presidents' souls. Bless me they're all rust up an atwist like some ol' boat brought up on shore an left t' fall apart. Why even the devil'd get lost inside one of them souls, they're so twist up an bent. (*Sentimentally:*) A boat like that ain seen the sea since the day the little boy who owned it forgit how t' smile. (*Smiles and nods.*) Tch tch tch . . . (*Laughs again, then calms herself.*) Sam I want the soul of a simple man. I don't say the soul of an innocent man — there ain no such article an I followed Adam an Eve out the garden so I should know. I'll send you a simple man. An you sell me his soul.

SAM. Holdee. There's a catch somewhere. Why don't you jist wheel right up t' him in your ol' folks-chair an buy his soul in the regular way?

GRAN. He's too god-darn simple. I tried it once. Soon's he see me his eyes misted up an he say 'Sorry I ain got nothin t' give you ol' lady, I'm hungry too'. I said 'Son I've come t' give you the fat of the land'. He said 'You sure are crazy with hunger' an went an stole a doughnut off the street stall an give it to me. I didn't turn up my nose at the doughnut. I've bought men for a crust of bread. I've bought up empires for a crust of bread. So I ate my doughnut. But hangdog he's so simple I couldnt git my hands on his soul nohow — jist the doughnut, which ain really the same. He take such pity on me — bein ol' in a wheel-chair an puttin on I'm hungry — I keep gettin these terrible terrible waves of lovin kindness well over me. I tell you boy I was almost fumigated. Lordee brrrr! An I would love his soul so. Dearly. If'n the world was one great Nigger Foot Pie I'd give it all away for that soul. An you know how I like my food. (*She is lost in secret contemplation. Suddenly she looks up sharply.*) You've always had a real mean look in your eyes.

SAM. I have?

GRAN. That's a devil's compliment. They don't come lightly. So you jist look deep down in his eyes — jist once — an you'll set up all sorts of twinges in there — a little hate, bitterness — you know how it is — a little suspicion — an his soul's gonna pop right out into your hands. You hold onto it real fast — an sell it at the soul auction.

SAM (*sniffs suspiciously*). Huh. All the pie an silver fish an

territory goin — ? (GRAN *nods*.) No. I still want commission.
Ain workin less I git commission. I act as your agent I'm
entitled to commission.

GRAN (*smiles*). Lord-bless-us-boy you git me that soul an you'll
have your ol' gran smilin an fawnin on you all the rest of the
days of the world. If'n that ain the sweetest commission ever
offered on this mortal earth I never sat down in front of Nigger
Foot Pie an gave thanks to America.

SAM (*touched*). Why bless you you sweet talkin ol' lady.

SAM *seals the bargain by kissing* GRAN's *forehead*.

GRAN. Now this is what you do. You git power over this soul
an sell it at the auction — an the moment he die his soul drop
straight into my hands. Now I'll hide up out of sight boy, or
the moment he see me he'll start mistin up an wellin out those
waves of lovin kindness an so help me I'll bring up — an the
devil bringin up in a wheel-chair ain a purty sight. Git on with
your fishin, an act nonchalant. (*She produces a large square
loaf*.) That's bait — for him not your fish. Look him full in the
eye an when his soul jump — give him the bread.

SAM. How'll I know him?

GRAN. He's the simplest fella you ever saw (SAM *goes to nibble
the bread*.) Leave that boy! Tch tch nibblin your own bait's
as bad as eatin next year's seed corn.

GRAN *wheels herself out*. SAM *takes up his rod and fishes*.
PAUL *enters. He is exhausted and in dirty rags. He sings as he
wanders by the river*.

PAUL.
Lawd I have a hollow chest
How the wind he howl in my hollow chest
He whistle in my hollow chest
Like a beggar man call his dog

Lawd I'm dressed in ter'ble rags
How the wind he love my ter'ble rags
He dress his-self up in my ter'ble rags
An dance like he's dancin for the lawd

Lawd I have these bare bare bones
How the wind he play with my bare bare bones
He done rattle my bare bare bones
Like he nailin down the coffin of the world

Lawd I work in the cotton field
This cotton field clothe half of the world
This white white sheet is my winding sheet
When the lawd he done fetch me home

Lawd I travel by the water side
I sings like a bird and I hops an glide
The river can't sing but it still roll on
I wonder do it know the direction of the tide?

PAUL *stops in exhaustion.*

PAUL. I'm a blackman. Don't tell no lie. My carrier bag was full of air. Then it got a hole in the bottom an the air fell out.

SAM. You hungry boy?

PAUL. I'm hungry suh. That's how I know I'm alive. Day I stop feelin hungry I know I'm dead.

SAM. That's a real intelligent line in conversation you got there nigger. I'm partial t' society talk.

PAUL. Yes suh. (*On the point of passing out.*) Sometime I pick my teeth t' try an git somethin t' eat.

SAM. You look as hungry as that ol' grey ice peelin off the top of the mountain. Bet you're so hungry your teeth have forgot how t' handle food. Have t' teach em all over agin. A for askin. B for beggin. C for chokin. Never did git t' D. Left school early. You ain lookin at me nigger.

PAUL. No suh.

SAM. Why not nigger?

PAUL. Dont know suh.

SAM (*produces the loaf*). Try keepin your eyes off that. Ever seen a loaf as big as that nigger?

PAUL. That's a big loaf.

SAM. This sort of loaf's got mighty good bread inside. If this loaf had feet it'd make a handsome Bread Foot Pie with Crusty Toes.

Off, GRAN *laughs.*

PAUL. There's that ol' river again.

SAM. Nigger you're saliverin so bad my loaf is startin t' blush. That's a white loaf, boy, with feelings. You're offendin my

loaf jist standin there oglifyin. Men been strung up for less.
Here nigger, you want my loaf? (*Strokes the loaf.*) You hear
me strokin my loaf boy? My my that crust make a purty
sound. Hmm mmm. You like the sound boy? That sound's
called succulence. When you sink your Nashville Tennessee
teeth in, that loaf's gonna sigh. Always did notice one thing: a
hungry man's got smart clean teeth, untouched.

PAUL. It's a purty loaf.

SAM. She's succulent. Like bread ought t' be. Sweet an
wholesome as mother made it. Don't suppose you had no
mother. It was all nigger t'gither in the dark church one
Saturday night an when the sheriff struck a match they all
vanish — an you was jist the little bundle left by the altar rail.
Well hangdog see here, my loaf still ain got no marks of the
tooth in it! A whole loaf an no mouthful rip out the side yit!
What smell better than a loaf willin an ready t' be eat up? I'm
askin a hungry — I said hungry — man.

Off, GRAN *laughs.*

PAUL. There's that ol' wind agin.

SAM. This crust's so crisp I can't stop my fingers atappin it for
sheer joy.

PAUL. What you want for that bread whiteman?

SAM. Nothin.

PAUL. I'm so hungry I'm gettin hallucinations.

SAM (*shrugs*). Nothin's what I said. That's the way I'm made.

PAUL. Whiteman ain made, he's a compromise.

SAM. What you mutterin t' yourself black boy?

PAUL. My teeth was chatterin.

SAM. You jist get them chatter on a slice of my hunky white loaf.
You don't use t' touch no white hand, you ain never gonna
touch no white woman — but you can *swaller* my white loaf.

PAUL. What do I have t' do whiteman?

SAM. Look me in the eyes.

PAUL. No.

SAM. Ain askin for a day's labour, ain even saying lift your finger
— jist your eyes.

PAUL (*shivers*). Ain lookin in your eyes.

SAM. Too like lookin in the sun? I understand that blackman. Only, you look me in the eyes an I'm gonna smile. How handsome you're gonna feel when a whiteman smile courteous on you nigger.

Off, GRAN *laughs*.

PAUL. There's that ol' water-fowl flyin in t' nest.

SAM. Hot diggety. You ever feel your life's manipulated by the clouds? I do. Never look up in the sky these days. I ain lookin in no distortin mirror. (*Holds out the loaf.*) I'm respectable an I give to charity.

PAUL. Said no man.

SAM (*cries*). Ouch. Dear o lor. My! Calamity strikes you down anytime. Knowd I should-a-never mentioned sky.

PAUL. What's up man?

SAM. Somethin in my eye. Ain no speck a dust. More like a whole sack full.

PAUL. Ain nothin in your eye.

SAM. There is. Right in.

PAUL (*still not looking at him*). Then why you starin at me like an eagle that's lost its mountain.

SAM. Ouch. My! Can a man stand so much?

PAUL. Ain nothin in your eye. Is there?

SAM. Nothin. Jump on your bike an peddle off like you was humpin your ol' grandma. It's niggers like you give the rest of the black race a bad name. Jist leave me in the ditch boy. By the river, anyroad. I go blind, that'll make you happy. Put you one up on a blind beggar. *You* beg but you ain blind.

Off, GRAN *laughs*.

PAUL. Must be a waterfall round the next bend.

SAM (*cries*). Boo hoo.

PAUL. You really got somethin in that eye?

SAM. No, I go blind for kicks.

PAUL. Thought it was the other eye jist now.

SAM. That's cause you ain lookin properly.

PAUL. An there ain no tears.

SAM. Tears? You're the sort a nigger expects the whiteman t' bleed t' prove he's had his hair cut.

PAUL. Your face is sure screwed up an ugly.

SAM (*aside*): I'll lynch the bastard. (*To* PAUL:) Ain you never seen agony before? Knew all them moaning spirituals was a fake.

Off, GRAN *laughs*.

PAUL (*tears a corner from his vest and offers it*). Here. You stop cryin now.

SAM. Can't stop cryin you stupid son of a bitch. (*Aside*.) I'll swear at him a little so's he don't git suspicious.

PAUL. Take my rag. You can dig that piece a dirt out yourself.

SAM. Can't even see t' find my head!

PAUL. Well you look up steady an roll your eyeball out of sight under your eyelid — an I'll hook it out. Lordee your holla'in go right through my soul.

SAM. Don't mention that word. I'm cryin enough already.

PAUL *pokes at* SAM's *eye with the piece of vest, but he doesn't look at him directly.*

PAUL. Still now.

SAM. Ouch.

PAUL. Well this here's difficult. I ain gonna look in your eyes man, so I jist have t' poke about a little.

SAM. Hell boy the way you're gettin it out's gonna blind me!

PAUL. Hold still.

SAM (*turns away*). Get back t' your walk. Gangarene'll set in and it'll soon be over.

PAUL. Is it that bad?

SAM. Enjoy your walk.

PAUL. Turn round man. (SAM *turns*. PAUL *looks in his eye*.) Don't see no dirt — only — (*Stares*.) Hey . . . look . . . at . . .

SAM *puts his loaf in* PAUL's *hands.* PAUL *takes a convulsive bit. He bites on a big silver butcher's hook. He pulls it out.*

PAUL. I bit on a butcher's hook.

GRAN *wheels herself on.*

GRAN. Hi ya folks! Hope they bin entertainin you. Blackman you're real black on black. (*Takes the silver hook from him.*) A silver hook with the tooth mark in it. My receipt. Take him to the soul auction Sam.

GRAN *wheels herself out.*

PAUL (*touches his chest*). I have a terrible pain here.

SAM. Boy you're gonna have a terrible pain everywhere.

Scene Two

Auction.

Attendants erect the auction block and give SAM *a mallet.*

SAM. On the block negree.

Attendants put PAUL *on the block.*

SAM. Now here's a fine specimen of black negreehood, you Nigger Foot Pie lovin folks. Sure he's a little shop soiled an bewildered right now. Maybe you wanna keep him around an fatten him up a little 'fore 'n you chop him up for pie. Jist let him run loose in the back yard an he'll soon plump out for slaughterin. My gran's been bakin Nigger Foot Pie all her life. Brung up a family of sixteen on the best Nigger Foot Pie you ever tasted. My ol' gran say he's got the makins of the best Negree Foot Pie that ever was. Biddin starts at five dollars. Thank you mam. Think how the kids are gonna holla when you come home with a fine nigger trussed up under your arm. Ten dollars. Thank you mam. Ever thought this could be your ol' folks' last Nigger Foot Pie Day? You wanna make it somethin t' remember don't you? Fifteen dollars. Thank you mam. I hope you folks are listenin real good now cause I'm gonna tell you what's special bout this here nigger. This nigger's got a soul — and that soul's thrown in with the carcase. Twenty dollars. Thank you kindly mam. That boy's got so much soul it's embarrassin. Twenty five dollars! Thank you

mam. My my my all that soul for a few dollars! Now I don't
want all you ladies astampedin t' git him in your larder. What
am I offered for this nigger body an soul? Thirty dollars mam.
Done!

Attendants collect PAUL.

Now Jake you take that negree down t' despatch an spruce
him up some. The customer gits our personal guarantee card
on every sale mam. If that don't make the best pie an pickled
backbone you ever chumped on, we buy back at sale price —
minus the cost of any meals you've had off him, of course —
but don't you worry none because you jist ain gonna bring
him back. Our complaints department gits so little work we
turned it into a Nigger Pie Cookery Demonstration Centre. (*To
attendants:*) Thank you boys.

The attendants remove PAUL *and the auction block.* SAM
goes back to the river.

Three

River bank.

SAM *casts the rod.*

SAM. Hot diggety. Now all you little silver fishes, I wanna see you
fightin t' hop on top of my hook. (*Slight pause.*) Come on
little fellas. (*Silence. Throws the rod down and calls:*)
Grandma!

 GRAN *wheels herself on in the chair.*

SAM. Gran I'm scandalized. An ol' lady like you has no place t'
go breakin her word even if she is the devil.

GRAN. Whatever you holla'in boy?

SAM. You done give me your word if'n I sell that negree body an
soul I get all the silver fish my heart desire.

GRAN. Sure I did boy.

SAM. Well dammit I sold him sure 'nough an I still can't catch no
fish!

GRAN. Then somethin ain right somewhere. I fixed it up — had
the lawd agree if ever I get that negree's soul up for sale then

all the little fish 'd jump ahoppin in your net. Why boy he said you'd have t' fight em off.

SAM. All I know I sold him for thirty silver dollars — an you ain gettin none a that till I get my fish.

GRAN. Why boy you ain gonna begrudge your grandma runnin that coinage through her ol' hands are you? That money buyed a soul, an I appreciate things like that. Sure you're gonna let my ol' fingers feel the blood on those coins. Ain you? Listen how my poor fingers ache. (*Cracks her fingers.*) Crick crick. Let them get a little warmin life off that soul-money boy.

SAM. No.

GRAN. If I weren't in this goddam chair I'd push you in the river you sassy fox.

LADY 1 *comes in. She wears Bermuda shorts, sun vest, big floppy sunhat and dark glasses with diamante frames.*

LADY 1. Come t' collect my nigger.

SAM. They're jist sprucin him up in the packin department mam. Our store never sends out a dirty nigger.

LADY 1. Cant wait all day boy. I gotta be gittin home to supervise the decoration of the house for Nigger Foot Pie Day. (*To* GRAN.) I sure like t' keep up all the ol' traditions. Can't trust no one t' hang out a few coloured tinsels an purty floral sprigs.

GRAN. You done buy my son's nigger mam?

LADY 1. Yes grandma. Here's my dollars.

GRAN. I'll take them sister.

SAM. I can manage dear. (*Takes the dollars. Chinks them.*) Real purty noise.

GRAN. Allus said you should have studied music as a boy. (*To* LADY 1:) You got yourself a bargain with that nigger.

LADY 1. Paid good money for him.

GRAN (*sighs*). Yes suh, that's what it sounds like.

Attendant brings PAUL *in.*

LADY 1. There's my purchase at last. I'm off. Sure is a novelty havin a nigger soul. Gonna show him all round our neighbourhood. Guess most folks ain even heard about souls. Those ladies are gonna be green. Gre-en. They ain gonna look down on me no more cause I ain got my college background. Ownin a nigger soul — why I expect that's better 'n majorin' in philosophy — wouldn't you think? That's why I want the whole place done up purty. Does my soul have a name?

SAM. Call him boy. Give em names an they gits above theirselves.

LADY 1. Well the problem don't arise for long. Sure as t'morra's Nigger Foot Pie Day he goes in the pie dish. My Horace is back home right now sharpenin up our carvin set. (*Embarrassed modesty.*) It's got real teak handles — we only use it special. I'll have my work cut out restainin Horace long enough t' let me parade my nigger round the neighbourhood. Then — in the pie! I'll show folks I ain afraid t' lash out an put a whole soul in my pie. I ain never begrudged no one nothin of mine, even if it cost money.

LADY 2 *comes in. She is identical with* LADY 1 — *same size, same clothes. They're like twins.*

LADY 2. Where's my nigger? Is this here my nigger? Your store sure takes time t' do a bit of spit an polish. They've had long enough t' pull you ready for the oven an give me your lights in a little carton like the best stores do. Well that ain your fault nigger. (*Pays* SAM.) Thirty dollars. (*To* PAUL:) Pie Eatin Day's comin so let's hit the road.

LADY 1. Now holdee mam. This here's my nigger.

LADY 2. Your nigger? Ain this the nigger with the soul?

SAM. Yes mam he have the soul.

LADY 2. Then that's the nigger I buyed a while back.

LADY 1. I can understand your confusion sister. All them niggers look alike on purpose. However this here is my nigger. I was jist acarryin him off when you arrived. Fact is if 'n I hadn't been exchanging the courtesies of the day with this sales-gentleman here I'd already have him back home crispin in the oven. We always celebrate Nigger Foot Pie Day in style in our house.

LADY 2. Well you ain gonna have much style this time less'n you git yourself a new nigger. Your cupboard is gonna be bare sister.

LADY 1. Now you take your hands off my nigger or so help me you'll be bare sister.

SAM. Now holdee holdee holdee. This ain no way of behaviourizin on the eve of National Nigger Foot Pie Day. I'm scandalized sisters.

LADY 1 or 2. Did you or did you not sell me that nigger — with one soul?

LADY 1 or 2. No.

LADY 1. Ain I the customer that claimed him first?

SAM. Tell the truth I don't know anymore.

LADY 1. Last time I ever shop this end of town.

SAM. Well the pair of you jist take your money an I'll keep the nigger. (*Offers coins.*)

GRAN. Holdee son. O lawdy dear you see what you done boy? You sold the same negree t' two ladies — an that crafty ol' lawd up there's been asniggerin an aholla'in t' himself all this time over the savin of one nigger boy's soul 'count of a double sale ain no legal transaction an — (*Suddenly realises.*) Or . . . ? Come here nigger.

PAUL *doesn't move.*

GRAN. Come an look me in the eye.

PAUL. No .

GRAN. I knowd it! He still got his soul. If he'd lost his soul he'd look me in the eye. Man he'd look clean through me. I know that ol' look.

LADIES 1 and 2. *Huh huh.*

GRAN. Nigger you're a cheat. An son — you're an idiot. You ain never gonna git that soul now. Why he ain gonna trust you no further'n an adder trust a polecat on a bicycle. You ain never gonna git him t' look in your eye agin — an he's so simple there jist ain *no* other way t' git his soul. Why that ol' lawd up there is a holla'in an ahootin with laughter. You ruined Pie Day for these good ladies an you done throw a dark cloud over the rest of your grandma's days. She'd set her heart on that negree's soul an now she ain gonna git it noways.

SAM. Shucks gran.

LADY 1 or 2. That's tragic.

LADY 1 or 2. Tragic though really. Ain cried so much since the dog bit grandpa when he hung him in the barn.

GRAN. Now I'll have t' spend Nigger Foot Pie Day mumblin on a bowl of nigger slops. Can't even chew the crust, so there's no way I could git my tooth in the bone. The flesh is willin but the jaws is weak. An then I'll rock myself t' sleep in my ol' rockin chair an that means the whole house'll have t' keep quiet as the tomb! An nothing no one's gonna say's gonna comfort me none. No nothin.

SAM. Aw gran.

GRAN. So don't try givin me none of your honey lip boy, I'll jist spit.

GRAN, SAM *and* LADIES 1 *and* 2 *go out.* PAUL *is alone.*

PAUL (*by the river edge. Calls*): Hey boy! (*No answer.*) Where that soul go? I looked in the whiteman's eyes an I felt you curl up like somethin in the fire. It was so long an grey behind his eyes an I looked an felt you jip up in me like a humpity horse but I jist had t' state — it went back so far inside his head like there was an old wide wide plain stretchin way off till it come t' the edge of the sky but there weren't no sky there jist the bars of a cage. (SAM, GRAN *and* LADIES 1 *and* 2 *come back quietly upstage.* PAUL *doesn't see them.*) An slap bang in the middle of that plain was the whiteman hisself, kind-a some little black shrivelled up apple fell out a dead tree and lied there in the desert. (*Calls.*) Hey boy. I'm callin you child. Here now. You come home or I'm gonna git cross. Well there you are child! Hidin under that bramble bush. You don't have to hide around now. That ol' white devil's gone home with them two white ol' she-goats, and that ol' white widder devil in the chair's givin em hell.

PAUL *picks up his soul. It is a large black doll decorated with coloured sequins.*

You bin frighted right out of me boy. Now I gotta find how to git you back in.

PAUL *sees them watching him.*

SAM. Thought you said that nigger was simple?

GRAN. If he saw himself in a mirror he'd step on one side to let hisself pass.

SAM. Don't look simple sitting there with his soul in his hands when good money's changed hands for it.

GRAN. Jist let me git my hands on it! I'd rip it up in two an you ladies 'd git half each. Half a soul's better than an empty oven any Nigger Foot Pie Day. I brung up a large family and know what it is t' go without. Times we ain had a nigger toe t' pass round and nibble on Foot Pie Day. But we managed an still had some laughs. Hell when I git t' talkin bout the bygone days I lose all track of where I'm at. Yes, if I git my hands on that nigger soul —

SAM. Why that's easy gran. Sit right there an I'll bring it to you.

SAM *goes towards* PAUL. *The soul rises and hangs in the air.*

GRAN. Son ain you learned nothin yit? That there soul is free-floatin. If you ever got real close t' that soul it'd whizz off faster than a bandycoot goin out the barn door when a tornado come in the winder.

SAM *goes back to* GRAN.

PAUL (*Calls*): Here boy.

The soul floats down to him.

PAUL. My you're a smart soul boy.

LADY 1 or 2. Don't seem right. No ways. A soul floatin round like that an we ain got the missile capacity t' bring it down.

LADY 1 or 2. Man sitting there with his soul in his hands. Why I'm sure the Reverend Michael Claythrob'd call that worse'n indecent exposure. He's special particular bout anythin dirty.

GRAN. Well this ain never gonna git Nigger Foot Pie Day off the ground. (*Wheels a bit closer to* PAUL.) Now lookee here Negree, you're stuck there with your soul in your hands an that's a mighty uncomfortable situation to be in for any length of time. Why that soul'll need so much nursin an carin you're gonna be wore to a frazzle. I almost feel sorry for you nigger. But silver dollars passed hands over your soul an the devil is a lady who keeps her word. You're in possession of stolen goods. An brother that ain good for your soul.

PAUL. Get lost ol' woman.

SAM. Listen here son none of that negree-talk t' my grandma.

LADY 1 or 2. Yes dear you ain jist some ol' woman none. You're a dignified matriarchal figure we're all proud t' love.

LADY 1 or 2. An you dress with such style. I wanted t' cry out loud when I first saw you. You may have noticed how I give an educated sort of gasp an jist clawed my throat a little instead. Why Mr Raymond — he's the guy I have fix my clothes — he's studied education too an he'd be bowled over by your simple homespun flair.

LADY 1 or 2. Likewise my Mr Stanley. I don't have no one t' fix my clothes. I have a coo-too-ree-ay. Mr Stanley doesn't jist speak French, he can do the gestures too.

GRAN. You galls are so kind I wish you was my daughters. (*Takes* SAM *aside.*) See here son I'm gonna arrange a soul-fightin contest between you an the nigger. Winner take the soul.

SAM. Holdee holdee. He's younger'n me.

GRAN. True boy, but he ain ate for so long, bin wanderin out all weathers, an breakin them wicked ol' jail stones — bet he's so hollow inside it'll be like shadow boxin.

SAM. Don't like it.

GRAN. An I'm referee.

SAM. Well the moment he start roughin me up you call a truce t' commemorate Foot of Nigger Pie Day.

GRAN. Won't be necessary son. (*Goes to* PAUL.) Here boy my grandson challenge you to a soul-fightin contest. Winner git your soul.

PAUL. Ain fightin.

GRAN. You wanna keep your soul don't you?

PAUL. I got my soul.

GRAN. My my.

PAUL. You come any nearer an my soul's gonna shoot up agin like a drownin man goin for the air.

GRAN. Nigger you really are the simplest nigger that ever was. Now here the devil can teach you somethin. Don't you know — listen now boy — if you don't fight for your soul that soul is gonna rise up one day an say 'Man, I quit. Don't belong here no more.' You don't appreciate your soul? You listenin boy? You think you can sit by the river forever with your soul for company? Ain that way at all. You lost your soul once boy, next time it ain never gonna come home — and you'll go straight in the next sizzlin hot Foot Pie that come along — an we'll all say grace and eat on that. You think I'm tellin lies nigger? Ask your soul.

LADY 1 or 2. Why you speak so reverend mam an look so sassy an dignified you almost sound like the Reverend Jeremiah Grace.

LADY 1 or 2. Or the Reverend Graham B. Knell for instance.

GRAN. Thank you sisters. You're charm itself.

PAUL. How d' you hold a soul-fightin match?

GRAN. That's so simple it ain even gonna bother you nigger. It's a duel with this here soul for weaponry. Jist take turns t' crack each other cross the head — or elsewhere where it's injurfiable, ain nothin gainst nothin in my book of rules. The one that pass out or give up through a busted back or somethin horny like that — he's knowed as the loser.

PAUL (to his soul): Sounds hard on you boy. I guess you'll jist have t' understand. If I'm ever gonna lose you in the end — hell I'll make a fight of it now. So don't you whizz off. I need you fella. (To SAM:) Where's the ring?

SAM (expansively). We're in the ring boy. Don't you know I'm always in a cage? That'll do me.

A cage is built round them. It's not too high to jump or climb over. A suitable way of building the cage would be for the attendants to unroll a length of chicken wire over part of the stage.

GRAN (aside to SAM while the cage is built): Sam I wanna give you my good luck charm. This here lead truncheon I carry in the top of my stocking. (She takes the truncheon out.)

SAM. What you carry that there for?

GRAN. What goes on under the devil's skirts is the devil's secret. Now every time your turn come round wrap that up in the soul an smite like the lawd done smote the lesser races! Ain a-castin aspersions on your own muscular powers. But I always find a good lead truncheon help you keep your balance. ,

SAM. Hee Hee. (*Sudden idea.*) Suppose he sees me with it!

GRAN. Sleight of hand boy! Remember how they shewed you pick pockets in Sunday School.

PAUL. Who git first crack?

SAM. We toss. (*He throws up all the silver dollars.*) Heads!

LADIES 1 and 2 (*looking at the coins*). Tails . . . tails . . . tails . . .

LADIES 1 *and* 2 *mutter as they search through all the coins. They are all tails.*

SAM. Doggone it gran! Can't you do better than that?

GRAN. Why here's a coin stuck under my foot. Rolled over on account I was tappin my foot with satisfaction — I do enjoy a soul-fightin match — an got stuck under that ol' shoe of mine. Well well. (*Examines the coin closely.*) Now what is . . . ? Eyes is a powerful burden when you git ol. Young folks don't always make allowance. Well I declare! that's — (*Looks up.*) What's that you holla'ed out boy? My hearin ain none too good neither.

SAM. Heads.

GRAN. That's heads.

SAM *takes the soul, wraps the truncheon in it and hits* PAUL *over the head.* PAUL *staggers.*

LADIES 1 and 2. Yarhoo! Whoof whoof whoof!

GRAN. Never seen sparks fly out a soul so fast.

SAM *removes the truncheon and throws the soul at* PAUL's *feet.* PAUL *picks it up.*

PAUL (*to his soul, quietly menacing*). Wow boy you sure have soul power! (*He lets the soul drop a few feet in front of him in the direction of the wire and crawls after it on his hands and knees.*)

LADIES 1 *and* 2 *whistle.*

GRAN. Why that blackie's yeller.

SAM *picks up the soul, hides the truncheon in it and spits on his hands.*

SAM. Should have fetched my gloves.

SAM *brings the soul down on* PAUL's *head.* PAUL *sprawls on his hands and knees.*

PAUL *(sings, quietly menacing):*
Lawd I have a hollow chest
My legs are weaker than the grass.

SAM *removes the truncheon and throws the soul to* PAUL.
PAUL *picks it up, lets it fall a few feet in front of him and
crawls towards it.*

SAM. It's beneath my dignity to fight this yeller coon.

GRAN *(sings):*
Nigger Foot Pie don't I love you
Nigger Foot Pie don't I love you

LADIES 1 and 2 *(whistle).* Call this a fight? I want the manager!
Where's the state governor? Just pulp that coon up and spread
him on the grass like sasparilla sauce. Grrr-yowww!

SAM *hides the truncheon in the soul and hits* PAUL *on the
head.* PAUL *buckles.* SAM *removes the truncheon and throws
the soul to* PAUL.

PAUL *(picking up his soul, quietly menacing).* O soul trust me.

LADIES 1 and 2. What's he a-sayin? Holla out loud nigger.
Wanna relish every word how you mutilate the language.

PAUL. Git on soul. *(Again he drops his soul a few feet in front of
him and crawls after it.)*

LADY 1 or 2. Wished I brung my drum-majorette costume an my
silver-dusted equipage. Feel in the mood for stompin an
hoofin an high steppin. Yessir I rise in my spangle dress like a
shootin star.

LADY 1 or 2. Wished I brung my native tom-tom set. When I'm
done up in my paint an totem feathers the turkeys they
screech! When I beat the hide off my tom-tom that don't
boom that howl!

SAM *picks up the soul and hides the truncheon in it.*

SAM. Hee-hee! *(To* LADIES 1 *and* 2:) Guess I'm doin you folks
a favour. When oven time comes round you won't have t'
hammer this steak. That'll be so tenderized it'll drip off the
fork. Think I'm gonna whack him cross the shoulder blades
so it don't git monotonous. Blades make mighty good pickin

at the end of a meal.

SAM *hits* PAUL *over the shoulders.* PAUL *pitches forward. He's now close to the wire.* SAM *removes the truncheon and throws the soul to* PAUL.

LADIES 1 and 2. Yow-ee! Yippee — yippee!

PAUL *picks up his soul.*

GRAN. My my that stuffin must wince. (*Laughs and dabs her eyes.*)

PAUL (*to his soul — quiet menace):* Not long now.

GRAN. I relish a soul-fightin match.

PAUL *rises to his feet and throws his soul outside the cage.* GRAN *gives a piercing scream.*

GRAN (*gurgles*). Lawd devil take him! (*Splutters and faints.*)

SAM (*looks at* GRAN). Have she got one of her heads again? (*To* PAUL:) That's agin the rules.

PAUL. Your turn boy.

SAM. Ain goin out there.

PAUL. Sisters you'd better attend t' that ol' woman. She's mighty sore bout somethin.

LADIES 1 and 2 (*fussing round* GRAN). Old fashioned clothes! Can't tell what's buttons an what's brooches. Ought-a have Raymond here. My these ol' weeds pick up dust! Mr Stanley would decline to touch them. They ought-a be in a museum. That's scheduled for demolition.

SAM. Nigger git there an bring that soul in so's we can git on contestin.

PAUL (*mocking*). Boss I's pretty poorly. You'll have t' give me a hand over the wire.

SAM. Be quick.

SAM *helps* PAUL *to climb out of the cage. Then he dusts his hands.*

PAUL (*outside*). Thanks boy. Now bless me I clean forgot whose turn come next . . .

SAM. You ain forgit. You jist climb back in here with that soul . . . an . . .! Gran said you was simple, I trusted you! Goddarn it you ain got no right t' cheat!

PAUL. Come an git my soul boy.

GRAN *splutters and froths as she comes round.*

SAM. You know I ain never been out the cage my whole life!
Git wind an everythin else out there. You'll fall in the river an
I'll sit back in comfort an watch you drown on TV. You come
back here nigger!

PAUL. Gran won't let you out to play? Git told off if you catch
your pants on the wire!

GRAN (*gasps*). Leave me sisters. Niggers an god is the cussed most
evilest things this side of hell — (*To* SAM:) an you is the
stupidest.

SAM *walks up and down inside the cage hitting himself with
the truncheon.*

SAM. Goddarn it! Beat by a nigger! Hot diggety! Lettin the white
man down! Panderin t' black hoodlums!

PAUL *picks up* SAM's *rod. He puts his soul down beside him
and starts to fish.*

PAUL. Jist look at all them silver fish a-twinklin in the river. I'm
gonna feed you up on the best silver fish fry you ever blinked
at son.

LADIES 1 and 2 (*scrabbling for the money*). If Nigger Pie's off
I'll drop down t' Deladio's Store an buy me a cast-off babe.
Hear they have some real sashy redskins. Marked down t' clear.
Try somethin in the yeller line. Time we dropped Nigger Foot
Pie Day an celebrated Yellow Curry with Redskin Side Dish
Day instead. Nigger flesh ain real fancy eatin no more. Jist lay
on your stomach and grumble. My dollar sister. Mine. Mine. I
bite a piece out of all my coins to showed they're mine. So do
I! (*They start to leave.*) Where you bite your coins? On top.
Hang-a-dog-for-santa-week like me! Can't you do nothin
original sister? Lookee here woman that's my coin. Mine I said.
I know the scar my tooth leave like I know the hoof of my
hound. (*Both* LADIES *produce a set of large false teeth with
orange plates. They are identical.*) Hey my spare teeth! You
got mine! — an we have bank guards on the bathroom!

The LADIES *go out.* PAUL *has caught a shoal of little silver
fish.*

PAUL. Lookee that!

GRAN (*to* SAM): Wheel me away t' Senior Citizens' Glades. Ain livin with you no more. You're dangerous.

SAM. He's got my rod gran.

GRAN. The lawd'll send a rod boy. An I'll apply it.

SAM *wheels* GRAN *out.* PAUL *sings.*

PAUL:
    Little silver fish for my soul an me
    Dancin t'gether in the bright blue sea
    A golden apple bouncin on the tree
    Pick it an eat it an you will be free

    When the river's as wide as it is long
    It'll be a sea for ships to sail on
    When waves are as high as the sea is broad
    They'll flush out the devil an drown the lawd.

    Now here's the moral of this here show
    Wise man said long time ago
    No man step in the same river twice
    Why the fish his world just flow away!
    Ain no knowed way of making it stay
    How's your world folks? You snug in bed?
    Once every day your world stand on its head.

The Swing

A documentary

The second part of A-A-AMERICA!

Author's Note

The end of Scene Two of *The Swing* should be played as a farce.
The farce begins when Skinner says 'Not till the day I die'.
Because the scene begins quietly and realistically the actors may
find it diffcult, in earlier rehearsals, to play the end as farce.
Nevertheless they must, with all the stylized speaking and
mechanical movements that go with farce. Why? Because I want
to show that the white characters are not passive victims of
tragic fate. They may not fully understand who they are and
what they do, but they are still responsible for both these
things. They murder on one special day because every day they
are greedy, arrogant, exploitative and — as all such people must
be — afraid. They commit their final great injustice because even
when they sit quietly on their porches and watch the sun go
down their lives are rooted in injustice. In this way they create
their own fate, turning themselves into monsters.

Like many people in the twentieth century — like whole nations
and classes — they may one day stand in bewilderment at what
they have done. But at least they can understand and be
responsible for the injustice of their daily life and their city: not
to say when they oppress and exploit that 'that is human nature'
but that 'that is what *I* do' . If they enjoy the benefits of an
unjust society, and seek their security in maintaining it, then
they are responsible for the great injustices that always follow
from little injustices. Those who sniggered at the broken
windows of a Jewish shop in 1933 are responsible for
Auschwitz. They made the building of Auschwitz possible —
just as they did the destruction of their own homes. We, too,
are responsible for the injustice of our daily life — and therefore
for the nuclear bomb sites that our leaders build. Those bombs
will be used to destroy our enemies and ourselves unless we

change our society so that we may live justly.

In the end injustice always leads to catastrophe. That is the clear lesson of history. Our species has no other alternative: either we live justly or we destroy ourselves. The world no longer provides a secure refuge for the unjust, we have made our weapons too strong and our societies too interrelated for that.

Why do people passively accept Auschwitz and nuclear death camps? How can our judgements be made so warped and our sensibilities so deadened? It's partly because the injustice, aggression and exploitation that we accept in small things blinds us to the nature of the great injustices that they lead to. The great catastrophies of history are the products of people's ordinary lives, of the way they earn a living and maintain their societies: *products* of that ordinariness not terrible aberrations that occur when things go wrong. That's why 'ordinary decent people' do on occasions such terrible things. They can only avoid responsibility for these by changing their daily lives — and that means changing the society in which they live: whatever anyone does to himself he hasn't changed his life till he's changed his society.

So the killers in *The Swing* are responsible for what they do and we won't help anyone to understand how they could do it by trying to give their lives the dignity of tragedy.

The formal farce ends with the end of Scene Two. The play then returns to realism. True, what happens then is a sort of farce — but it is not farce used, as at the end of Scene Two, to explain and analyse what is shown. The events in Scene Three happened, in essentials, in life, and are neither tragedy nor farce. They are the farcical-tragedy of the ordinary and must be played as realism.

An actress who based her performance on a character's psychology might try to find the meaning of Greta's madness in the imagery she uses when she goes mad. This wouldn't help the actress to understand Greta. Most acting is still based on the idea of the soul, or psyche, as being like a white rabbit a magician pulls out of a hat; or on the idea that a person can be compared to a mysterious house out of the door of which people are always coming but into which no one ever goes. But I write on the premise that people don't live in a certain way because they have a certain psychology but that they develop a psychology that enables them to live in the way they do. Character is the subjective habits we develop to enable us to live according to the ideas we accept as useful and true. You don't change people by changing their characters but their ideas.

Americans don't go to psycho-analysts because they have psychologies that prompt them to. They go because they think their problems are less pressing and fundamentally different from that of a man dying of starvation. They are wrong. Men don't live by bread alone and whatever else it is they live by— Americans are starving to death for lack of that. A man dying of lack of bread will tell you that he doesn't have a personal problem but a social one. He has no food because his society cannot (or will not) feed him. Thus those who starve for lack of bread know their situation better than the affluent know theirs: Americans still think their psychological problems are personal and not social. They go to church to be 'born again' not because they have a psyche, still less a soul, that prompts them to. They go because they don't want to change their way of life ('the American way') and are born into a 'new life' so that they can go on living the old one in the same old, American way. A sort of cultural schizophrenia which can never be the basis of justice.

Greta's imagery shows she's mad but not, except in a very superficial way, why she's mad. To understand why she's mad you must return to what I said earlier. She's driven mad by the ordinary, daily life of her town. If we watch Skinner behind his counter, if we watch him writing in his ledgers and locking-up his shop to go to church, we can tell there will be mad people in his town. Greta becomes mad because she has no economic power and this makes her vulnerable. It means that she has less social activity to disguise her madness in — in the way that Skinner does so well. She is neither a worker nor an employer and so there are few people it pays to share her views of the world. This means that they have little chance of being accepted as ordinary, normal views. So she is vulnerable and insecure and when in time the injustice of her town produces — as it must — catastrophe, she goes certifiably mad. But Skinner's madness is greater: he is politically mad, he suffers from the farcical-tragic madness of the ordinary in an unjust society. All the other white people in the play share this madness. Fred as much as the others — as Paul could easily point out. I don't know whether Greta was raped in the yard. Whether she was or not makes no difference to the play. I know the good, honest, decent, ordinary white citizens of her town destroyed her mind.

The Swing was first presented by the Ambiance Lunch-Hour Theatre Club at Inter-Action's Almost Free Theatre, London, on 22 November 1976. The cast was as follows:

Black

PAUL (28)   Don Warrington

White

SKINNER (53)	Glyn Owen
RALPH SKINNER (17)	Kevin Elyot
STAGEHAND 1 (42)	Ron Travis
STAGEHAND 2 (19)	Garry Whelan
STAGEHAND 3 (26)	Kenneth Ryan
FRED (26)	Roddie Smith
PHOTOGRAPHER	Gilbert Vernon
CLOWN	Henry Woolf
HELEN KROLL (54)	Liz Smith
GRETA KROLL (32)	Illona Linthwaite

Directed by Jack Emery
Designed by Norman Coates
Lighting by Suresa Galbraith
Sound by Pete Mount
Wardrobe by Monica Strauss

The action takes place in Livermore, Kentucky, USA, in 1911.

Scene One

A theatre. A simple swing of wood and rope hangs motionless from the flies. It has been decorated with bright paper flowers and bunting. There is a pile of props — cut-out trees and birds, folded hangings and so on.

PAUL comes on from the wings. He is black.

PAUL. In the fall of nineteen eleven in Livermore Kentucky a blackman was charged with murder. He was taken to the local theatre and tied to a stake on stage. The box office sold tickets accordin to the usual custom: the more you paid the better you sat. The performance was this: people in the pricey seats got to empty their revolvers into the man. People in the gallery got one shot. An pro rata in between. Course he died very easy compared t' the style of some lynchin's.
What you're gonna see is substantially true. We thought it right t' give the plot away. Obvious, if there's gonna be a lynchin you'll sit more comfortable if you know exactly what seat history's sat you on.

PAUL starts to pack up props. He works silently and efficiently at his own pace. MRS KROLL comes on. She's in a bad mood, but she doesn't let much of it show. She stands in silence for a moment. Paul works as if she wasn't there. She sits on the swing but doesn't move it.

MRS KROLL. Home, profession — gone. Vamoosh. (*Sings.*) 'Life is a milliner's show . . . ' (*to* PAUL:) That's a wonder: know something?

PAUL (*going on working*). No Mrs Kroll.

MRS KROLL. I didn't fall off this swing last night and have the doctor saw my leg off. Really bring the last curtain down. (PAUL *works in silence.*) Go tell her make coffee.

PAUL (*puts some props down*). You could send some of the bits and pieces to the school.

PAUL goes out. MRS KROLL looks at the props. SKINNER comes in. He has a bunch of flowers. PAUL goes in and out with the props while SKINNER and MRS KROLL talk.

MRS KROLL. Why hello! O flowers! How divine of you. You shouldn't have.

SKINNER. Drove by the churchyard an nip cross the wall an found a fresh one.

MRS KROLL. Now they're lovely and don't you tell lies. O dear! I'm going to cry. You've been to Beaumont and Wains and I do believe you were a real beau and asked Lillian for my favourites. (*Smells the flowers.*) Heavenly. (*Sighs.*)

SKINNER. It's a new life Helen. All the things you ever wanted to do — now's your chance.

MRS KROLL. What things?

SKINNER. All the things woman — I don't know! Mrs Skinner's always sayin if she only had the time . . . Travel!

MRS KROLL. Too old to travel.

SKINNER. Ain true.

MRS KROLL. Paul put these lovely flowers in water would you? I'd go out of my mind if they withered before their time. (PAUL *takes the flowers with him next time he goes out.*) O I'm not complaining. I'm too old for vaudeville. Some of the boys out there could be my grandsons.

SKINNER. Accordin t' my book they look up t' you.

MRS KROLL (*shrugs*). That's not what boys buy tickets for. Nice of you to think of flowers. If you're going go fast. Soon's we're out of this place I'll be fine. Never have sat in the corner and wept.

PAUL *comes on with a ladder. He unfastens the swing and drops it to the ground.*

MRS KROLL. She fixing coffee?

PAUL. Told her agin.

MRS KROLL. Nothing more dead than an empty theatre in the morning, is there? (*Stares out front.*) Worn patches in the plush. Soiled seats. (*Grimace.*)

SKINNER. I'm takin over. They tell you?

MRS KROLL. This place?

SKINNER. That's right.

MRS KROLL (*confused*). They didn't tell me.

SKINNER. This town's gonna boom. If they only find half the coal they're talkin about — we're still gonna boom. The company's stipulatin for three hundred more miners next year. An families. They're plannin t' pave the sidewalks in the centre. Now's the time to expand. I'm openin up a new store right here. Fine frontage. Best part of town. I'll have my warehouse here in the back.

MRS KROLL. Got the freehold?

SKINNER. Two year lease. Go cautious first.

MRS KROLL (*looks out front*). Well it could have been an abbatoir.

SKINNER. Haw haw. (*Stamps on the stage.*) Make a fine cellar down there.

GRETA *comes on with a tray of coffee things.*)

GRETA (*cold but polite*). Good day Mr Skinner.

SKINNER. Good day Miss Kroll.

GRETA. I brought you a cup. Paul told me you were here.

SKINNER. Real kind. (GRETA *pours.*) Did you see the cut flowers I brought your mother?

MRS KROLL. Heavenly.

SKINNER. Let on I'd been robbin the churchyard. Haw haw.

GRETA. Milk?

SKINNER. Always say the corpses can kick up their own. Haw haw.

GRETA. Sugar?

SKINNER. Jist the three.

GRETA (*hands him a coffee*). There.

SKINNER. Thankyou, thankyou.

GRETA (*pouring coffee*). How is Mrs Skinner?

SKINNER. Fine, fine. I'll tell her you ask. She'll sure —

GRETA. Coffee mother? That's nice Mr Skinner (*Hands a coffee to* MRS KROLL.)

SKINNER. My your coffee sure is a cup-an-a-half.

GRETA. Pocohontas. I have it mailed in.

SKINNER. Real good stuff. Think I might try stockin some. Pricey I suppose?

GRETA. I really wouldn't know Mr Skinner.

SKINNER. Ah no, no,

GRETA (*finishing*). There.

MRS KROLL. Don't leave all the packing to Paul. Have you packed your books yet?

GRETA. All except the two or three I'm reading.

SKINNER. You read more'n one book at a time?

GRETA. That's called studying Mr Skinner.

SKINNER. My my!

GRETA. There's more Pocohontas when you're ready for it.

SKINNER. Much obliged Miss Kroll. (GRETA *nods and smiles*.) Suppose you'll have time on your hands.

GRETA. Now I wonder why you should suppose that?

SKINNER. You won't be helpin your ma t' run the theatre.

GRETA. O I've never helped her —

MRS KROLL. That's true.

GRETA. — much in the theatre. My work keeps me busy.

MRS KROLL. If you're counting on living off Sitting Bull coffee you'd better forget your work and get a job.

GRETA. Don't you think mother made a fine light commedienne Mr Skinner? People never knew the effort it cost. Mother has quite exhausted herself for years. (*To* MRS KROLL:) Thank heaven you're going to get the long rest you deserve.

SKINNER. Yup, stock up a few packets an see if they move.

GRETA (*turning to go*). I'll leave it there for you to serve yourselves.

SKINNER (*stopping her*). Ralph — my son Miss Kroll.

GRETA. Yes?

SKINNER. A good lad. Helps fine in the shop. Ralph's mother never have t' tell him anything twice.

MRS KROLL. Sounds a model kid.

SKINNER. School ain done him much harm but it ain done him
much good. He hardly know more'n me an Mrs Skinner.
Speakin to an educated person, it won't be out of place if I say
that ain enough.

GRETA. Come now.

SKINNER. Thank you Miss Kroll. I knew you'd understand. Now
I know your time's precious — only I was hopin you might
spare a bit of it t' git Ralph educated up.

GRETA (*refusal*). O I'm sorry Mr Skinner.

MRS KROLL. What a heavenly idea! I've always told her she was
a school-ma'm.

GRETA. I'd like fine to help. Knowledge has no meaning 'less it's
passed on to the young. But . . .

SKINNER. Yup — I want him t' talk jist like that.

GRETA. My work . . . Our situation is unique. We live on the
border between civilization and barbarism. Which way shall
we go? Do we know the answer? I see it as my duty — to
posterity — to record our lives — in all their colour and shades.
The chiaroscuro of history. I keep a diary Mr Skinner. Even
the words we're exchanging now will be touched on in it.

SKINNER. Well I'm honoured. I shall sure tell Mrs Skinner that
I'm goin in a diary. And you're gonna change your mind for
Ralph's sake.

GRETA. Why Mr Skinner I really think I've made my decision
very —

SKINNER. This town's gettin a new class of citizen. Educated
people like yourself. Their needs have t' be catered for. I
intend t' open a new store — an run the old one for the miners.
The two class of folk don't wanna mix. I'll run the miner's
store myself — I'm rough enough for them. But Ralph — he's
kinda clean an lean. I'd like him taught so's he can carry on
like you did jist now — bout civilization an so on. He came
out with that he could sell a real classy line of goods.

GRETA. We must not despise the practical benefits of education.

SKINNER. I envisage the sort of store that pulls in the money
end of the market. Chairs for people t' sit on while they're

bein served. A pot plant on the counter maybe. Y'know
the sort of store Miss Kroll. Course with people like that you
don't sell the bulk. But you git the turnover on the higher
prices.

GRETA (*refusing apologetically*). My work . . .

SKINNER. I know the best don't come cheap. I'll invest money
in my son. An you'll choose your own time. Ralph's no
trouble. We brought him up t' believe in manners. He know
how t' treat a lady.

GRETA (*takes his cup*). I'd like to help. Our young people so
desperately need guidance. There's so much low in their
backgrounds — they're pulled down by —. (*stops short.*)
I'm tempted. One couldn't do much. A little Latin and Greek.
Was it milk?

SKINNER. O please.

GRETA (*pouring*). And some Hebrew would be possible. Three I
believe?

SKINNER. Er —

GRETA (*puts in sugar*). Hebrew is a much neglected language.
Wrongly in my opinion. Those without it miss so much. I
would like Ralph to have access to the original texts at Bible
classes. No translation can give that Mr Skinner. The original
offers — well, the heart. O there are so many things I can do
for Ralph. (*Hands the coffee to Skinner.*) I wouldn't have
suspected you could realise that! He shall have the best. Light
light light!

SKINNER (*taking the coffee*). Thank you kindly. Now I —

GRETA. To think! (*Walks away from them.*) Here in this quiet
town, hidden behind the counter of a general provisions
merchant, is a young soul yearning to be touched, opened,
freed. I went in every week with my shopping list — and never
saw! How blind we intellectuals can be! Of course I had
noticed the sensitive white face, so shy and yearning. Not
unlike the dying Keats. What do you think mother? (*Walks
away again.*) And those delicate white hands. The long
tapering fingers on the scales. I'm sure he writes verse! (*Turns
to them.*) Yes — I will help! I must!

SKINNER. That's mighty handsome. Now the money can be —

GRETA. Arranged arranged arranged! The harmonium too. Is he musical?

SKINNER. You should jist hear him whistle when he git mad!

GRETA. I'll plan a whole course. No more time must be wasted. Books! He'll need grammars, primers, dictionaries —

SKINNER. Well — if it's necessary it's fine by me. Learn him t' talk good an I'll be happy. We'll skip the Latin an Greek. I aim for him t' talk t' customers better'n I can. Now he start spoutin Latin an Greek — they ain gonna understand him at all!

GRETA. But surely! The classical languages give a gentleman such a —

SKINNER. English'll do. An not *too* fancy. Jist fancy enough so's he sound real mean when he talk, like educated folk. So's it makes you feel hot an kinda embarrassed. If he talks t' the hands like that — he ain have no bother in keepin em in their place: they'll know they're in it.

MRS KROLL. It's a heavenly idea. And the money will be useful won't it Greta?

SKINNER. An you can help him catch up on his numbers. He give ol' Miss Leggit thirty cent short last Friday. Come back squarkin like a turkey-cock laid a square egg. I sub his money thirty cent. *That's* the sort of lesson he want taught. Sweat roll off me by the time I got shot of Miss Leggit. Thirty cent! Least that's the right way. How many times he give too *much*? They don't come hollerin back then. Couldn't sleep that night with the idea runnin through my head. Mrs Skinner got quite fiery!

MRS KROLL. That poor dear.

SKINNER. Always tell him it's your store one day, you'll *have* t' take care then.

GRETA. Ah, I've remembered. I'd decided to start a new series of papers on the effect of local geological structure on character. I shall have to disappoint Ralph after all.

MRS KROLL. Harry's an old friend, and you'll help him out.

SKINNER. I'll send him round t'morra an — (*Turns to* GRETA.) — you can decide.

MRS KROLL. She's decided. Send him today.

SKINNER. Well that's a weight off my mind. I mean, t' think he's got — (*Forgets.*) — culture. Move with the times! Remember the old days? Rustling, gun feudin, when a man got drunk he shot the town up's though that's as natural as spewin. We formed the Citizens Committee of Justice Riders. Soon stamp it out. Time was a man didn't know if he cussed he wouldn't be strung up on the pole. Soon had law an order. Hope that go in your diary Miss Kroll. Now I'm the last t' complain bout all the new developments hittin town. But new industry mean new folks, strangers who ain familiar with the ol' ways an can't respect em. That means hooliganism. Law breakin. Who rob the bank last year? We git thievin out the store. White boys too. (*To* PAUL:) Ain jist Blacks, White, who had advantage. Funny: good always bring the bad. Paint the wall an someone'll write dirty on it. Ain bin no justice ridin round these parts for fifteen years. Bit of colour trouble but that's somethin else. Look at him — (*Indicates* PAUL.) — tryin t' look innocent. But we never broke up the Justice Riders. (*To* GRETA:) If there's any taint of the hooligan hid up in Ralph you're gonna chase it out of him. That matters t' me an I'm grateful. If he don't do his lesson right, I'll back you up. Still hang the harness strap up in the kitchen dresser. I've larrupt him till he salute the flag an step off the sidewalk for a lady.

GRETA. Good manners are next to —

SKINNER. Right on. An numbers an the art of speakin rhetorical t' customers. But no Latin an Greek. We're a general stores an we don't git no call for that. Good day ladies. Mrs Skinner's mindin the shop.

MRS KROLL *goes with* SKINNER *to show him out.*

PAUL (*indicates the tray*). Finished?

GRETA. I wonder if mother knows she's a bad actress? O I'm not a holly Anna. You can't study the classics without knowing what men are for. But to expose her little routines up here! It's the betrayal of my father I mind. Night after night. He'd never let her go on stage when he was alive: knew too much about talent. He never wanted to go on himself. It was all he could do. But his *mind* — I know something of *that*. That was on better things.

PAUL (*puts cups on tray*). I'm takin these through.

GRETA. The moment he died up she hops, dancing — well,

tripping — and singing, and she never thinks she's dancing on
his grave. And so badly. He must be turning — and the only
one of them in time with the music.

PAUL *goes out with the tray.* GRETA *goes up stage, turns and
comes down reciting.*

GRETA.
  O lord Apollo
  Come come come and speak the truth at last!
  How often I, Electra, asked
  Offering my cheap offerings, all that I could buy.
  Now I come with all I have:
  Veneration and longing!
  To ask, to beg, for aid.
  Help us to show men
  How well the gods reward their crimes.
  Show war and blood-lust running side by side
  To the fixed end.
  Let the hunters into the murderer's house!
  None shall escape!
  Wake dreamers to the sound of ropes!
  See! the spokesman of death
  Creeps in the rich old mansion
  Armed with —

GRETA *stops. A young man has come through the audience.
He is tall and thin, with short crinkly fair hair. He wears a blue
denim suit, a white T-shirt and a floppy white denim hat. He
carries a tray covered with a cloth. He supports the tray with
one hand, takes off his hat with the other and puts it on top
of the tray.*

FRED. Gee I'm sorry ma'm. Didn't know you were rehearsin.

GRETA. The theatre's closed.

FRED. That's what I thought. 'S why I didn't —

GRETA. I'm not rehearsing. What is it you want?

FRED. See Paul.

GRETA (*calls*). Paul. (*To* FRED:) Why?

FRED (*lifts tray slightly*). Show him this.

GRETA (*calls*): Paul!

  Slight pause.

FRED. Sorry t' butt in . . . (*Pause. Suddenly:*) Great guy Paul!
Teached me a lot.

GRETA. Teached?

FRED. Electricity.

GRETA (*confused*). O. Lights.

FRED (*whipping his index finger through the air*). You're there.

*Silence. GRETA turns and walks off. FRED comes up on
stage. He carefully sets the tray on the ground, kneels by it,
gives a little clap of excitement and rubs his hands together.*

FRED (*quietly*): Yow-eeee . . .

PAUL comes on. FRED whips the cover from the tray.

FRED. Ta ruummmm!

It is a large plain white icing-cake, covered with very large candles.

PAUL. . . . Your birthday?

FRED. Naw stupid! *Diploma* Day!

*FRED presses a switch on the cake stand. The candles light up
with flashing coloured lights.*

FRED (*quietly*): Yow-eeee! Will yer look at that!

PAUL (*honestly*): Great man.

FRED. My gall bake the cake an I fix the wirin. Hell man ain you
notice yet?

PAUL. What?

FRED. The lights! They go zing-zing-zing-zing-boom! (*Stares at
PAUL. No response. FRED makes a deprecating gesture.*)
Aaaahhh! I'm a graduate of the Ernest Webster
Correspondence College of Electric Science. With honours!

FRED and PAUL shake hands.

PAUL. Congratulations Fred.

FRED (*pumping PAUL's hand*). I owe the honours to you.

PAUL. No man you're just plain smart.

FRED. Right on! — but you sure helped me a lot. Guy says —
I have a letter signed by the President of Ernest Webster
College — I'm the sort of pupil give electricity a good name.
He says: go forth young man an prosper!

PAUL. When do we git t' eat it?

FRED. We don't git. I'm preservin that for posterity. Know what them lights are sayin?

PAUL. No.

FRED. Y' don't know everythin. Them lights is codified lights. Morse — least I learned somethin useful at the Band of Hope. You'd've learned too if they let blacks in. Them lights is flashin out a message to the United States! That cake is announcin to the world: FRED OSPENSKY IS CUTER THAN THE WIZARD OF OZ!

PAUL *laughs*.

FRED. Yow-eeee! I'd stand on my head if I didn't have t' act respectable like a son of Ernest Webster College!

PAUL. You're a fool man.

FRED. Say that agin.

MRS KROLL (*off*). Paul!

FRED. Hell why d'you stick them two ol' maids? Me? — quit! Now you listen Paul. Me an the gall's puttin by every cent we git. Couple of years we're gonna start a little shop. Electric installation. Repairs. Apparatus. This town's growin so fast y'have t' run t' keep up with the suburbs. Come in with us.

PAUL. You crazy?

FRED. What you don't know bout electricity belong t' the age of the candle. Hell I can't *risk* leavin you out!

PAUL. Ospensky blacks don't git t'jobs like that.

FRED. I worked it out. Course you don't go out installin an Dorothy keep the counter. You stay out the back an do all the real work — them bad, bad repairs make my head ache. Hell folks'll think you jist mind the babies — which we'll have by then.

PAUL (*unpersuaded*). So you encourage uppity niggers. What Dorothy say?

FRED. Hell you know women on anythin like that. I'm boss. (*Brightens up.*) Right on! I'm boss! Leave it t' Big Fixer!

MRS KROLL (*off*): Seen Paul Greta?

PAUL (*smiles*). You're so stupid one day Dorothy'll give you the push.

FRED. Don't be like that Paul. Black ain what it was.

Things change.

MRS KROLL (*off*). Greta?

PAUL. They don't change that easy. Not for anyone. You git
    fixed on the past like you pumped it into your arms. It's a
    terrible habit t' shake. One day your people are gonna lynch
    each other in the gutter over a drop dime.

FRED. It's Diploma Day. Ain rowin.

PAUL. You'd better go out the back.

They go off. The stage is empty.

Scene Two

GRETA's *room. A round table. Books.* GRETA *sits at one side of
the table.* RALPH *at the other.*

RALPH. The one who's all hassle. This ain right, that ain right.

GRETA. Isn't.

RALPH. Yeh. Nothin's right. Two minutes later his girl follows
    him in. They don't know each other. One hassles an kicks up
    a stink an the other drops half the store in her coat linin.

GRETA. You have to keep your eyes open.

RALPH. Sure do have to.

GRETA. And what d'you read?

RALPH. No time t'read. Pa says read. Soon's I sit down with a
    book he say git up you lazy — do this, do that.

GRETA. But you can read?

RALPH. Sure I can read! I read Forty Thousand Leagues Under
    the Sea by Jules Verne. That's a good book. You ever git t'
    read that? I read that at school.

GRETA. Today you're going on to Virgil.

RALPH. Wow! . . . Virgil, isn't he some sort of Greek?

GRETA. Latin.

RALPH. Only pa said for me not t' —

GRETA. In English translation.

RALPH. Well pa said for me —

GRETA. Now Ralph. There's no need for your father to know what we study. Frankly your father is a — well never mind. I don't want you to discuss our work with anyone. You're a young man. You must start making your own decisions.

RALPH. Okay, okay. If you say so Miss Kroll.

GRETA (*looks at the time on her fob watch. Opens the book*). A very extraordinary thing happens in Book Two of the Aeneid. Troy is burning. Aeneas the Trojan hero addresses his father. (*Reads:*)
'The fire-ball comes raging through the town
The rolling blast of furnace heat.
Up on my back, dear father —'
(*Explains:*) He was old.
'—I'll carry you on my shoulders.
The burdens we love are light! We must chance our luck
And run through the burning city.' So I lifted my father
Onto my back with hands still —

What are you looking at Ralph?

RALPH (*nods*). That.

GRETA. My fob? You have good taste Ralph. My father Reinhart gave it me. He brought it with him from Germany. It was my grandmother's. Fine isn't it?

RALPH. Yeh.

GRETA (*holds out the watch. The chain is still fastened to her dress*). The engraving will interest you. Mountain gentian. We will be doing botany. The silver's so fine and delicate. Touch it. Feel: soft, burnished with touching.

RALPH (*touches the fob with his finger*): Yeh.

GRETA. It's my proudest possession perhaps. Well — shall we get on? (*Reads:*)
'The burdens we love are light! We must chance our luck
And run through the burning city'—
(*Explains:*) To escape the Greeks.
— So I lifted my father
Onto my back with hands still red from war.
My son twined his fingers in mine and ran at my side
With his short steps. My wife came behind.
We kept to the —

She stops. RALPH *is still staring at her. Slight pause.*

RALPH. Never heard such a quiet tick.

GRETA. Almost silent. It was made in Chamonix high up in the European Alps. Ruskin mentions it in Praeterita. The air up there is so clear and the craftmen sit in their windows. They need light for their delicate work. Centuries of craftsmanship and history and struggle ticking by in a little watch. Don't you like the story?

RALPH. O it's fine.

GRETA. Please like it. Try. If there was one person I could share these things with — (*She stops. Puts the book down. She speaks with a light voice.*) The ancients were dry? They were passionate, angry, questing! Our lives on the frontier are so like theirs — and so different. We have the violence and killing — my own father was killed — but what else? They had the lyre — we have the banjo. Wine — the four-ale bar. Attic drama — vaudeville. Aeneas' son saw men killed — so have you. But what else have you seen? You haven't even seen the naked body! Because everything else is ugly, that's ugly! Aeneas' son saw the naked body. We cover ours — like you put blemished fruit at the back of the store. Don't some of them wash? Ralph have you — as your teacher — tell me — did you ever see a woman's breast?

RALPH. Well —

GRETA. No.

RALPH. Er — kinda — the lads — once —

GRETA. I'm not ashamed to ask a young man that question. What is education? For god's sake! — how to read invoices and weigh up soup powder? Can't you see this strong man with his father on his back, tears streaming down his old beard, the little boy running to keep up, his wife hurrying behind. The trackless waste. Their city burning. Murderers foraging for refugees in the long grass. Doesn't that say *anything* about the human condition? Ralph! (*As she reads she slowly uncovers one of her breasts and takes it out.*)
We reached the gates of the city,
An arch of fire and through it a world on fire.
My father said 'Faster! Run! See their shining armour!
The flashing bronze!' In the panic and haste
I lost my wits! We ran from the city streets

Out in the open fields. Then — O terrible!
My wife was gone.
Did she stop running because fate meant to rob me?
Fall with weariness — and not shout for my help
Because she wanted me to save my father and son?
Or lose her way in the smoke? It is not known.
We never say her again. If I had looked behind —

RALPH. It's beautiful.

GRETA. You think that?

RALPH. Let me touch it.

GRETA. No.

RALPH. Miss.

GRETA (*gently*). How firm the nipple is. It glows. It means I
like you Ralph. When the lady's breasts are firm it means she
likes the man. Always remember. The sign of fondness.
(RALPH *stands*.) Now you've seen what Aeneas and his son
saw. Sit down. (RALPH *sits*.) Now. Your turn. (*Hands him the
book*.) Seventy two. It's marked.

RALPH (*reads*):
Did she stop running because fate meant to rob me?
Fall with weariness — and not shout for my help
Because she wanted me to save my father and son?
Or lose her way in the —

RALPH *stands*.

GRETA. I shock you.

RALPH. No, no —

GRETA. It's wrong?

RALPH. No! It's — I want to — let me —

RALPH *crosses to her. She stands.*

GRETA. Ralph. No. Sit.

RALPH *walks away across the room. She covers herself. She
sits.*

RALPH. I — think I'd better go home.

GRETA (*stands*). Your parents — father — you mustn't — don't
say —

RALPH (*alarmed*). God no no no! Hell. Jesus. No.

GRETA. No. (*Sits.*) We must understand our lives and then act as if we didn't. There are women Ralph — men go to. I understand them too. But we can't speak of them. We must be as silent as this book —

A tap on the door.

GRETA. Come.

PAUL *comes in with a lighted oil lamp. He puts it on the table.*

GRETA. That's very good Ralph. Go on. Thank you Paul.

RALPH (*reads*):
— If I had looked behind
To see she was keeping up!
I had not even thought of her till we came to the grassy hill
Holy to —

GRETA. Ceres.

RALPH (*reads*):
— where all the survivors assembled.
She alone was not there. Without knowing it, I her husband,
Her son and friends, lost her forever.

They both look up at PAUL. *He stands some way from the table waiting and watching them.*

PAUL. Was there anything else?

GRETA. No thank you.

PAUL *goes.*

GRETA. D'you like my oil lamp Ralph? I try to keep up the old ways in my room. I love this soft light at dusk. And the quietness. Strange evening. You mustn't think I've ever —

RALPH. No, no, no.

GRETA. How kind and good you are. I wonder if any other women will feel your presence as I do. Talk about yourself.

RALPH. O. (*Slight pause.*) I'm jist part of the store. Dad's had our name put right cross the big windows. Big gilt letters. And son.

GRETA. That's nice.

RALPH. Yeh . . . The fellas out the mine grin at me through the
 letters. Wet their fingers in their mouths an wiggle em in the
 air.

GRETA. We have to live with the sordid.

RALPH. That store's so dark —

SKINNER (*off*). Ralph! Ralph!

 GRETA *and* RALPH *stand.*

RALPH. That nigger! He's told!

GRETA. What? No! How could he?

SKINNER (*off*). Ralph!

GRETA. Sit! Books!

PAUL (*off*). Sir!

GRETA. Books. (*They sit and frantically open books.*) We must
 look as —. He couldn't have told. He couldn't. There's no time!
 Seventy-four!

RALPH. Seventy —

GRETA (*angrily*): Four!

 A moment's silence.

PAUL (*off*). Miss Kroll's room.

RALPH (*stands*). That nigger saw!

GRETA (*pulls him down*). Sit!

 Silence. SKINNER *comes in.*

GRETA (*rising.*) Why Mr Skinner have you come for a lesson
 as —

 She stops: she has noticed SKINNER's *torn clothes, bruised
 face, and his right hand and forearm crudely bundled into a
 blood-stained splint-bandage.*

RALPH. What in . . . ?

 PAUL *comes in behind* SKINNER.

RALPH. Pa! Sit down!

SKINNER (*stands. Gasps*). Son!

RALPH (*to* PAUL): Whiskey!

 PAUL *goes.*

RALPH. Pa — for god's sake — ?

SKINNER. Store. Broke in. Hoodlums.

RALPH. Ma?

SKINNER. Next door. Riders out. Called em out. Went for me. Smashed. Lootin hoodlums. The store. Cut. Look. (*Gasps.*) Aw god!

GRETA (*calls*): Mother!

SKINNER. Smashed windows. Spillin sacks. Tea chests. Ah better. Big window's smashed.

GRETA. How terrible! My god that blood!

SKINNER (*to* RALPH): Git back. Guard the store. God *I'd* better come!

RALPH (*pushing him down*). Stay there.

SKINNER. They'll burn the store!

RALPH. They won't. I'm goin.

GRETA (*calls*). Mother!

PAUL *comes in with whiskey and glasses.*

RALPH (*impatiently to* PAUL): Here!

RALPH *pours a drink, gives it to* SKINNER *and goes out.*

GRETA (*to* PAUL): Where's my mother?

SKINNER (*calls at door*): Mrs Kroll!

GRETA (*looking after* RALPH). Will he be safe?

PAUL (*to* GRETA): She's comin.

SKINNER (*gasps and splutters as he reaches for the bottle. Knocks his arm on the bottle. Half spills it. Shouts, then winces*). Aw! Ah!

GRETA. Spilt. O god. (*She mops up the whiskey.*)

PAUL. Let me do the —

GRETA. I can manage!

MRS KROLL *comes in.*

MRS KROLL. What in god's name is — (*Sees* SKINNER.) Harry!

GRETA (*angrily indicating* PAUL). Does he think I'm an idiot?

MRS KROLL (*to* SKINNER): What is it?

GRETA. Does he think I can't —

MRS KROLL (*to* GRETA). Shut up!

SKINNER. My store.

MRS KROLL. What?

SKINNER. Hoodlums.

MRS KROLL. On the streets? Paul put the front shutters up. (*She has taken the bandage off, she controls her shock*.) Then get Dr Load. How did they do this?

SKINNER. Hatchet.

PAUL *goes out.*

GRETA (*fascinated by the wound*). How awful! They could have killed him.

MRS KROLL (*to* GRETA): Hot water. (*Calls:*) Paul fetch the first aid from the box office.

GRETA *rushes out.* MRS KROLL *pours* SKINNER *a drink. She prepares the wound.*

SKINNER. My store, my store.

MRS KROLL. It's going to hurt.

SKINNER. Heard this gigglin. Knew Mrs Skinner wasn't back. Crep down in the dark. My little spy hole back of the shelves. Looked. Light from the street lamp. Saw some shapes. (*Drinks.*) Gigglin: thought — kids. Went in. Men! Come for me. Drag me on the floor. Held my head down. This guy stood on my hair. Can't move. Nailed there.

MRS KROLL. Still.

SKINNER. My store. Slashed the sacks an the insides ran out. Broke my bottles. Bringin things an smashin em by my head so's I saw — in the light from the street. Rip up rolls of calico. Thought they'd see the meat slicer. (*Suddenly bursts into tears.*) Aw god! thank chriss there's insurance.

MRS KROLL (*calls*): Greta! Quick! (*To* SKINNER:) Your wife?

SKINNER. Next door. Wednesday:plays cards. Run round when they left. Saw me — screamed. Aw god. (*Touches his scalp.*) It's bad . . .

MRS KROLL. A bit.

SKINNER. My store.

PAUL *comes back. He brings a first aid box.*

PAUL. Barricaded the front. Locked the doors. I'll git Dr Load.

MRS KROLL. Send that girl up! I need water!

PAUL *goes.*

SKINNER. Didn't see their faces. Strangers. Got their voices.

MRS KROLL *pours two drinks. They drink in silence.*

SKINNER. Someone has t' spoil it. Gets goin — then 'long they come smash smash smash.

PAUL *comes in with a bowl of water.*

PAUL (*quietly*): She ain in the house.

MRS KROLL. What? You sure?

PAUL. Street coat's gone. An her hat.

MRS KROLL (*subdued exasperation*). God almighty.

SKINNER. She go after Ralph?

MRS KROLL. I've no idea. (*Takes the water from* PAUL). Get the doctor.

PAUL. You all right on your own?

MRS KROLL. Yes, yes. Go on.

PAUL *goes.* MRS KROLL *talks as she cleans and dresses* SKINNER's *wound — almost as if she were talking to it.*

MRS KROLL. I hate this town. And I'll be buried in it. Didn't choose it. Just a stop on the vaudeville circuit. The lease going cheap — Reinhart said we couldn't afford to miss it. Only get the chance once. We put in all we had. A year later he was shot. Stupid. A bar brawl. He wasn't even involved.

SKINNER (*shaking his head in his hands*). My store.

MRS KROLL. Wouldn't let me see him in the bar. Waited at the police house till they brought him. I went in the bar on my way home. The huge mirror had fallen out of its frame. Smashed. Blood on it. Must have been his.

SKINNER. We strung up the guy that shot him. Still think of Reinhart when I pass the telegraph pole. Wish he'd had the satisfaction of knowin.

MRS KROLL. He never saw me act. He'd hate it. I'm not good. (*Shrugs.*) No money. Theatre lease I couldn't sell. What could I do? Now they don't come. Tired of the same old —

Off, a scream. They both hear it.

MRS KROLL. Her!

SKINNER (*stands*). The yard!

MRS KROLL. Quick!

SKINNER. Listen! Listen!

A moment's silence.

SKINNER. Nothing.

MRS KROLL. It is! You heard!

SKINNER. Listen!

MRS KROLL (*not stopping*). She screamed. The lane out the back.

SKINNER. We're on edge. It was a horse. An automobile.

MRS KROLL (*going*). All right.

SKINNER. Stay here!

MRS KROLL. You go!

SKINNER. The window! (*Opens the window off right. Pokes his head out.*) O hell there's a fire! Not near the store. Thank god. (*Calls.*) Miss Kroll!

MRS KROLL. Harry we must go to —

SKINNER (*head still out*). Will yer listen! (*Calls:*) Hallo?

MRS KROLL *goes out.*

(*Head still out.*) She's round the store with Ralph.
He'll see she's okay. What the hell she go out for any-road?
Wants her bottom smack. You let her do what she like. She put on any more airs the whole town'll laugh. (*Calls:*)
Miss Kroll? (*Suddenly realising.*) Hell someone could be out there with a gun —

He has turned back quickly. Sees MRS KROLL has gone. Curses silently. Pours himself a drink at the table. Picks up a book, leafs over a few pages.

SKINNER. My store . . .

He shuts the books and tops up his glass. GRETA comes in.

She carries a bowl of water, a clean towel and some medical dressings.

GRETA. Now Mr Skinner where is that wound?

SKINNER. Where you been?

GRETA. It must be washed. Every speck of dust must come out. That causes the trouble. Where's mother?

SKINNER. Out looking for you.

GRETA. O.

SKINNER. Ain you bin out? We heard somethin out back.

GRETA (*goes a few steps towards the window and glances out*). I hope she's all right. Should I go and see?

SKINNER. Goddam it no! The whole town'll be running round lookin for each other.

GRETA (*touches her forehead*). It's so silly. (*Looks at his arm.*) She saw to your arm . . .

SKINNER. Are *you* all right?

GRETA. The —. I'm worried for Mrs Skinner.

SKINNER (*pours a drink and hands it to* GRETA). Drink this.

GRETA (*shakes her head*). It fuddles my brain. (*Takes the glass.*) Perhaps . . . tonight . . . (*Drinks in silence.*) How very silly. (*Starts to fuss at the table.*) Books everywhere. Such disorder. (*She picks up some books and holds them futilely.*) Ralph. Such a promising —. I have high hopes. A natural talent for —. Of course undeveloped, but —

MRS KROLL *comes in.*

GRETA. I was telling Ralph's father. We must be proud — yes, I was most —

MRS KROLL. Where've you been?

GRETA. I'm sorry I took so long. (*Points vaguely.*) The water. Anything like this — I find so upsetting. Mr Skinner's been kind enough to —

MRS KROLL. Your coat was gone.

GRETA (*puts the books back on the table*). The whiskey. (*Starts to cry.*) How silly.

SKINNER (*reaches out to pat her*). Now you mustn't let —

GRETA (*big flinch*). Don't!

SKINNER (*mumbled apologies*). O I jist — you seemed —

MRS KROLL. What is it?

GRETA. I want to tear the skin off my hands! I want to tear my skin away!

MRS KROLL (*motions to* SKINNER). Outside.

GRETA. Filthy. Horrible. Dirty. (*Pounds the table.*) Unclean.

SKINNER (*going, bewildered*). What is it?

MRS KROLL (*to* GRETA. *Quietly firm*). Stop it.

SKINNER *goes out.*

GRETA. You don't know. You don't know.

MRS KROLL. I'm trying to find out. (*Pours whiskey and gives it to her.*) Drink it.

GRETA. No, no.

MRS KROLL *puts the glass in* GRETA's *hands and tilts it against her teeth.*

GRETA (*dribbles and drinks*). Oooo.

MRS KROLL. Well — out in the yard —

GRETA. Yes. Yes. Yes.

MRS KROLL. And?

GRETA (*face down across the table*). Nothing.

MRS KROLL. A man?

GRETA. What's the use —

MRS KROLL. A man was —

GRETA. Yes, yes, yes! (*Spits the words in her mother's face.*) A man! A man! Does it satisfy you!

MRS KROLL. Don't talk to me like that! What happened?

GRETA. I'm going to gag! (*She bends over a basin but only dribbles.*) Ah . . .

MRS KROLL. The man hurt you? Greta!

GRETA. What?

MRS KROLL. He assaulted you?

GRETA. It was dark. He put his hand on my mouth. Mother he ripped — (*Touches her breast.*) Here.

MRS KROLL. He pushed you on the ground.

GRETA. What?

MRS KROLL. The wall?

GRETA. My dress was torn. When I got in I found my watch was gone.

MRS KROLL. Greta you're not a child. I'm asking you: were you assaulted? Sexually.

GRETA. The wall? . . . He showed me his wound and I wanted to go out. Out, out. There was a fire out there! I went down the yard — through the gate — in the lane. I turned to the fire. Someone shut the gate behind me. I heard a noise. A hand came out of the dark and — (*Lies face down across the table again.*)

MRS KROLL. You *were* assaulted? (*Gestures to her own body.*) Here.

GRETA. I came indoors and my watch was gone. Ripped off.

SKINNER *comes back. He looks enquiringly at* MRS KROLL.

MRS KROLL (*quietly*). I'm not sure. I think she's . . .

SKINNER (*quietly to* MRS KROLL). A man?

GRETA. I won't go out anymore. Never. People will look at me like a dog running with its nose from ditch to ditch! An old maid who —. I won't go out!

SKINNER. We'll git the beast. (*To* GRETA:) Did you see anythin? (*To* MRS KROLL:) You? (MRS KROLL *shakes her head. To* GRETA:) Would you know his voice?

GRETA. Who?

SKINNER. He didn't say nothin? No, the swine knew what he was up to. Done it before. Some lad spur of the moment, he'd he'd've blurted out. 'Please'. 'Shut up.' This lad know what he's at.

GRETA. I suddenly saw my father in the dark. (*Picks up a book.*) I thought I was being murdered. Then it was all over. (*Looks at the table.*) So disorganised . . .

PAUL *comes in.*

PAUL (*slightly out of breath. Quietly*): No doctor. No one.
   They've gone into town. A gang started a fire.

MRS KROLL *takes* GRETA *out.* PAUL *starts to follow.*

SKINNER. Hey.

PAUL (*stops*). Whiskey Mr Skinner?

SKINNER. What you called now?

PAUL. Paul sir.

SKINNER. Right. (*Holds the bottle.*) Drop left. How long you
   worked for the Krolls?

PAUL. Fourteen year.

SKINNER. My how faithful you black race are. Must've seed you
   around but . . . (*Drinks.*) Some git sweet when they drink, rest
   sour. Right?

PAUL. Yes Mr Skinner.

SKINNER. Took your time.

PAUL. Don't follow your drift sir.

SKINNER. Dr Load.

PAUL. Knocked. Went round the back. Made sure his horse was
   gone. Then I waited a while. Knew that cut was bad. Doctor
   ought t' see that.

SKINNER. If niggers had blue eyes yours'd be blue. (*No answer.*)
   Follow my drift?

PAUL. Yes sir.

SKINNER. Step in the light boy. Wanna make sure I'll know you
   when the next fourteen years gone by.

PAUL. I'd better see if Mrs Kroll —

SKINNER. You ain shy?

   PAUL *comes close enough for the light to shine on him.*

PAUL. What's wrong Mr Skinner.

SKINNER. Aw — you tell me boy.

PAUL. I weren't round your store Mr Skinner. You know I was
   here when you come —

SKINNER. Who see you round the doctor's?

PAUL. No one. I don't think.

SKINNER. When you git back?

PAUL. I come straight up here.

SKINNER. Blue eyes an a smart tongue. They sure knock out a fancy brand of nigger round here.

PAUL. Mr Skinner it ain right for you t' —

SKINNER. Shut up! Shut up! Shut up! Listen nigger I've had the privilege of chasin niggers out that swamp — O I know where they hide up! — and the pleasure of bouncin em on the end of their braces strung round their neck. Up an down. In the good ol' days. Which ain passed yet!

Silence.

PAUL (*quietly*): I'm sorry they broke your store Mr Skinner an —

SKINNER. You make excuses for me? Shut up! Shut up! Shut up! You make excuses for *you*! You need excuses. What excuses you got? (*Silence.*) Now what you do when you come back 'fore you come straight up here?

PAUL. Nothin.

SKINNER. No detour?

MRS KROLL *comes in.*

No. None. Cause you never even went! You'd never have time t' go an then do what you done!

PAUL. What have I done?

SKINNER. Don't use words t' me.

PAUL. Could I go now Mrs Kroll.

SKINNER. Stay right there. At the wall.

MRS KROLL (*quietly to* SKINNER): Harry the funny thing is I'm —

SKINNER. Get her t' bed?

MRS KROLL. Yes. I'm not sure anything happened.

SKINNER. She ain said? (MRS KROLL *shakes her head.*) Next best thing t' caught in the act. Young gall — she wouldn't know the words.

MRS KROLL. O you can't live over a theatre and not —

SKINNER. If she did she'd never bring herself t' use em. I
wouldn't embarrass the lady by askin. Listen Helen: a man in
the dark? — a gall? Of course he did! What could *she* do?
Knowin your daughter — she's been brought up a lady, which
does you credit — she jist fainted. Probably don't even know
what happened.

MRS KROLL (*impatiently*): O! — (*Tries to keep calm.*) Perhaps
it was just — she lost her watch.

SKINNER. Robbery make it worse.

MRS KROLL (*becomes aware of* PAUL, *vaguely wonders why
he's standing at the wall*). Paul?

SKINNER. He ever give trouble before?

MRS KROLL. Trouble?

SKINNER. What is he? Some sorta saint?

RALPH *comes in with* FRED. FRED *carries his hat in both
hands.*

RALPH. Pick him up in the yard. Prowler.

FRED. I was not prowlin any! Hell what is this?

SKINNER (*to* FRED). You in the yard?

RALPH. Yeh.

SKINNER. Where you from?

FRED. Oak Street.

SKINNER. Miner?

FRED. Look I don't know you mister —

SKINNER. Why you prowlin in someone's private back yard?

FRED. I was visitin.

MRS KROLL. Here?

FRED. See Paul ma'm.

SKINNER. Why?

FRED (*shrugs*). Social call.

RALPH. Social?

SKINNER. Funny world where white man pays social calls on the nigger community.

PAUL. He don't mean it that way. I been teachin him bout electricity.

SKINNER. You sure are an unorthodox nigger. This nigger's teacher now. Don't teach niggers like bona fide niggers teach. He teach white. Not readin an writin an anythin good an wholesome like that. He teach the wonders of science! Nigger, this white man don't need you t' talk for him. He can talk for hisself. (*To* FRED:) So you pay a social call on the nigger with a little electric demonstratin throwed in on the side. What sort of a freak are you?

RALPH. Yeh.

SKINNER. Empty his pockets.

FRED. Now hold on.

RALPH *goes to search* FRED. FRED *pushes him off.*

FRED. Git off! (*To* SKINNER:) You ain got no right t' —

SKINNER. I'm a foundin officer of the Justice Ridin Committee. In my book that's *right.* You think before you reply: you tellin the citizens of this town you don't co-operate with them?

FRED. Hell no — I . . . ! (*Empties his pockets.*) Billfold. Handkerchief — (*Honestly:*) sorry the handkerchief's dirty ma'm. Smokes. My knife — wipe the blood off 'fore I come in . . . Come to tell Paul bout the fire.

SKINNER *picks up the handkerchief, stares at it a moment and puts it down without uncrumpling it. Nods.*

SKINNER. Son you got into bad company with this here nigger. Thank your lucky stars I step in an stop it 'fore you was mixed up in somethin real bad.

RALPH. Pa —?

SKINNER. Miss Kroll was raped by a dirty man t'night. Back up the yard.

RALPH. Jesus!

MRS KROLL. Well we don't know that Harry. I'd rather

we hoped —

SKINNER. Helen why don't you go and look after your little girl?

MRS KROLL. We don't know. Not for sure.

SKINNER. Dr Load will confirm.

FRED. Hey! You didn't think I — ?

GRETA *comes in. She wears a long nightgown and behaves like a child.*

GRETA. Could anyone tell me the right time? (*To* RALPH:) Have you the exact time on you please? Mother my watch has gone. I've lost my watch. Who took my watch? (*To* RALPH:) Why you staring? (*Cries.*) Father will be cross! Where did I put it down! (*To* PAUL:) Lean and clean doesn't wash. (*To* SKINNER:) Could you oblige me with the correct time? (*To* PAUL:) It's late! It's late!

MRS KROLL. Greta come to bed.

GRETA. Where-o-where is my little watch gone? (*Cries on her mother.*) Mother my beautiful silver watch.

SKINNER. What a terrible sight. I'll never let myself forget this.

GRETA. Look at your watches! Are they there? The watch thief is coming! (*Calm.*) Could you oblige me with the right time?

SKINNER. Not till the day I die!

The farce begins. MRS KROLL *pours herself a drink.*

RALPH (*weeps*). O god it's terrible.

MRS KROLL (*drinks*). She's my only child!

GRETA. It's late! Late! Late! Father will be cross! A clock tower striking!

MRS KROLL (*drinks*). I'm her mother!

GRETA. Where's the clock tower?

RALPH (*sobbing*). Gee god! Jesus Mary.

GRETA. The yard! That's where I lost my watch!

SKINNER. That poor kid!

GRETA. In the dark! At the gate! The yard! The yard!

MRS KROLL. Honey baby!

GRETA *runs out.* MRS KROLL *runs out after her.*

SKINNER (*violently*). Now I'll have my say!

RALPH. I'll git Dr Load.

PAUL. There's no need. He'll come as soon's he git —

SKINNER. You said no one was there!

PAUL. So I left a note.

SKINNER. A note?

SKINNER ⎱
RALPH ⎰ He left a note?

PAUL. In his door.

SKINNER ⎱
RALPH ⎰ In his door!

RALPH. If he left a note —

SKINNER. — in his door —

SKINNER ⎱
RALPH ⎰ He ain done it t' Miss Greta!

RALPH. It was someone else!

SKINNER (*to* RALPH): Get to Dr Load's. Find if that note's there! Knock the door down but find out if it's there!

GRETA (*off*): My watch!

PAUL (*looking through the window*). They're in the yard. Her mother's chasin her round.

MRS KROLL (*off*): Greta!

Off, a chicken squawks as it flies out of the way. RALPH *pours himself a quick drink.*

GRETA (*off*): My watch! If I don't wind it up it'll die! I know it'll die!

RALPH (*to* SKINNER): Sure you can manage while I —

SKINNER. Go! Go!

RALPH. Got it at home. (*Gives a pistol to* SKINNER.)

SKINNER. That-a-boy! Your pa's proud of you! (*They shake hands.*)

RALPH *goes.* SKINNER *pours a drink and empties his glass.*

MRS KROLL (*off*). Greta I'm hurt too! Can't you understand! (*A chicken squawks.*) I carried her. Fed her at this breast. It's all gone. Sold up. Theatre closed. Life finished. O Reinhart thank god you never lived to see me old!

SKINNER (*shouts through the window*). We won't forget Helen. You're hurt too. (*Goes to* FRED *and hits him with his unwounded hand.*) The mother's hurt too okay?

FRED. He's mad!

SKINNER. My son'll never be the same again. (*Calls:*) Drink! (PAUL *fills his glass.*) Look what you done to this family! (*Cries, pistol in one hand and glass in the other.*) An me a strong man weepin. (*Drinks and cries.*)

GRETA (*off, fading into the distance*): My watch is dead! Will no one help me to bury my dead? Ashes! Ashes!

MRS KROLL (*off, fading into the distance*): Not in the street! Not in your night dress!

PAUL *is backing away. The bottle hangs from his hand. He stares at* SKINNER.

SKINNER. An my store too! Animal! (*Hits* FRED.)

FRED (*white*). He's mad!

SKINNER. Beast!

Scene Three

A theatre. The vaudeville orchestra plays the orchestral version of 'I Wore a Little Grey Bonnet' (The Quaker Girl. Monckton). Three STAGEHANDS dressed in white overalls set the swing. MRS KROLL comes on in theatrical Edwardian dress. She carries a parasol. As the STAGEHANDS finish she sits for a moment on the swing and gracefully thanks them with a smile and and a bow of the head. Then she promenades as she sings.

MRS KROLL (*sings*).

Life is a milliner's show
Every young lady confesses
Even the quaker you know
Has to take care how she dresses

So when at home I went out for a walk
I had to mind that the folks didn't talk

> I wore a little grey bonnet
> Not a flower or feather upon it
> Always hidden my face would be
> 'Cause it was under my bonnet you see

> I wore etc.

So I was very demure
Folly and flattery scorning
All the young fellows I'm sure
Liked just to bid me good morning
They would come up as I went on my way
Saying it's really a very fine day

> I wore a little grey bonnet
> Lots of eyes were fastened upon it
> Though they wanted to look at me
> They couldn't peep under my bonnet you see

> I wore etc.

Once on a Sunday in June
Such a nice gentleman met me
Talked for the whole afternoon
Told me he'd never forget me
He couldn't see I was blushing so pink
I didn't know what to say or to think

> I wore a little grey bonnet
> All the time his eyes were upon it
> Then I found he was kissing me
> His face had slipped under my bonnet you see

> I wore etc.

Applause. MRS KROLL *goes off. She returns for a bow.*
SKINNER *comes on clapping. He is dressed rather formally:*
black jacket, white shirt, spotted bow tie.

MRS KROLL. You heavenly audience! It's been divine!

SKINNER. This really is the last appearance of Mrs Helen Kroll
on her own stage. Give her a big hand. (SKINNER *leads the*
applause.) Okay lads.

SKINNER *gestures offstage. The three* STAGEHANDS *come*
on. They lay protective sheets over the stage. They are

*nervous and this makes them brash. They grin at the audience
while* SKINNER *talks. One waves to a girl.*

SKINNER. Brothers an sisters. Citizens of this town. I'm glad t'
    see such a full house t'night. (*Spreads his hands.*) These hands
    serve you good people in the store. Wrap your bread, weigh
    your beans, measure your coffee. (*To the* STAGEHANDS:)
    I git in your way fellas tell me t'move. (*To the audience*:)
    These hands have held a whip an a gun. They've held men's
    legs while the noose was drop over their head.

AUDIENCE. Ya-haaaa! Wheeeeee!

STAGEHAND 1. Right on Mr Skinner!

SKINNER. Fellow Americans. How we run the law's the same
    how we live our lives. The store, street, law: one. Let the law
    slip: you git bad measure in the store and the sidewalk end up
    death-row for the good citizen. That's how it is!

Audience applause.

SKINNER. Law ain something above. We make it with these
    hands every day of our lives.

STAGEHAND. Jist a foot Mr Skinner.

SKINNER (*moves slightly*). T'night we ain ridin for justice in
    the dark.

Whistles and applause.

SKINNER. We're ridin in the footlights. There's nothin t' hide.
    We ain ashamed of doing what's right. I declare this stage t' be
    a hall of justice!

Applause. STAGEHANDS 1 *and* 3 *go.* STAGEHAND 2 *stays
on stage, folds his arms and listens.*

SKINNER. The good ol' Justice Riders — they were a group of
    brave, public-spirited men. Half the manhood of this town
    stayed at home in bed. Now I'm glad t' see most the whole
    town here! Barrin a few ol' maids who ain quick on the draw!
    I'm honoured t' see our venerable ol' gran'pappies. I'm proud
    of you young fellas ain yet out of school. I see many of
    you've got your wives an sweethearts an mothers along! Let's
    say a special hello to our ladies.

SKINNER *leads the audience in applause.* STAGEHANDS 1
and 3 return with FRED. *He has been dressed in a grey suit*

and pale shirt (no tie). He is roped. He is white with terror.
The STAGEHANDS *are nervous. They try to tie* FRED *onto*
the swing. He falls on the ground. Audience whistles, cheers,
boots.

FRED. Fellas. Please.

STAGEHAND 1. Hell.

STAGEHAND 2. Hold him, hold him.

STAGEHAND 1. Git the seat.

STAGEHAND 3. Billy.

FRED. Please. Please.

AUDIENCE. Hold his head up. He's shy.

Laughter, boots.

SKINNER. Like men we do our own work. Like honourable men
we git pleasure doin it. We know the sort of man don't git his
pleasure doin right. *He* git his pleasure doin bad.

AUDIENCE. Right on!

SKINNER. Friends. If this is wrong — it ain, but if — we done it
t'gether. We act and speak united. You're all in this. No one
man t' blame. The guilt's on all. No man can point out his
brother or pour scorn on his neighbour. Git your hands off
your butts — I know you're itchin t' go — an study your palms.
No lady I ain askin you t' tell fortunes. What's there?

HECKLER. Dirt!

SKINNER. Lines! Everyman's hand's much the same — an
everyman's hand's different.

STAGEHAND 2. Oughta hoist him up a bit.

STAGEHANDS 1 and 3. Wha' for?

STAGEHAND 2. Git his feet off the ground.

STAGEHAND 1 (*shrugs*). Okay.

The STAGEHANDS *raise the swing so that* FRED's *feet clear*
the ground.

SKINNER (*hands spread*). Yes brothers! The same but different.
God put it on our hands for a purpose. When we work, play,
pat our off-spring on the head, help the oldfolk, give the
hand of friendship, wave farewell t' the departed — (*Applause*

grows.) god put it right there before our eyes. The same —
members of one community: we owe it service an duty — but
different — each man has his own place an rank: with his own
tasks an ability t' carry them out. Law an order writ on the
palm of your hands as sure as Cain's curse was writ on his head.
(*Applause*.) Step out of line: you take on tasks for which you
ain got abilities. In my book that's anarchy: you cut off your
hands!

Applause.

FRED. You gotta stop him. You gotta stop him. He's mad.

SKINNER. Hey fellas stuff his mouth so's I can finish.

STAGEHAND 1 *gags* FRED. FRED *makes noises from time to
time and tries to shake the swing.*

SKINNER. This is how I've organised this do. Every ticket-buyin
member of this audience is entitled t' one shot. Them that paid
the higher prices git first shot.

Audience applause and boos. Cries of 'Shame'.

SKINNER. Pit, gallery, gods. Anyone step out of line, the
usherette ladies 've been told t' git their names. They'll hear
from the Committee. T' show this ain based on favouritism,
I give up my go.

Audience applause, 'Shame'.

SKINNER. Was happy t' do so.

WOMAN IN AUDIENCE. Can't shoot straight.

SKINNER. Git her name. Don't none of you red-necks complain.
You work harder you could afford first go. (*Applause, boos.*)
I'll tell you what I'm gonna do. Every gun-carryin man woman
an child in this audience is gonna git themselves a voucher.
That voucher is exchangeable for goods on the day I open my
new store — in the new one *or* the old one! That voucher's
worth fifty cents. Can't do fairer than that! (*Applause, cheers.*)
Now you won't often see prayin on stage. I'm gonna ask you
to join in an act of prayer. (*Bows his head.*) Lord god guide
our aim. We ain numbered 'mongst them mugger-lover folk
who think of the criminal all the time. We remember the
victims an their loved ones lord. Amen.

AUDIENCE. Amen. Right on. Yow-eee. Born again.

CLOWN *comes on. Long white face, bulbous nose, black hunting cap with long peak, black tail-coat, baggy trousers, long black shoes.*

CLOWN. Er Mr Skinner. Mr Skinner sir. Er beg your pardon Mr Skinner.

SKINNER. I'm busy here.

CLOWN. Did you say — er — did you say jist a while back —

SKINNER. Speak out son. I won't eat you. (*Aside to audience:*) Ain never be that hungry! (*Laughs.*) My new store go bust I'll git a job on stage. Haw haw. O indeedy!

CLOWN. Pardon me Mr Skinner. Mr Skinner sir.

SKINNER. Well son?

CLOWN. O . . . (*Mock modesty: slots his two hands together at the fingers, turns the palms down, straightens his arms and rocks his hands from side to side in front of his crutch.*) Could I have your go?

SKINNER. Could you have my . . . ?

CLOWN. Let me, let me, let me. (*Produces an old pistol.*) Look what I got.

SKINNER. What is that?

CLOWN. My brother's weapon.

SKINNER. What is your brother — deformed? Runs in the family.

CLOWN. This was used at the Boston Tea Party.

SKINNER. T' stir the tea? (CLOWN *cries quietly.*) I'm sorry.

CLOWN. I wanted t' help. No one lets me help. I know why.

SKINNER. Why?

CLOWN. There's something wrong with me. Something horrible, twisted, ugly, unnatural —

SKINNER. I wouldn't put it as bad as that!

CLOWN. O yes it is! I bite my nails! (*Bursts into tears.*) Mother always told me t' git my own lunch, Mr Doctor—sir.

SKINNER. Dry your eyes an have my go.

CLOWN. Thank you, thankyou Mr Skinner. (*Bobbing and bowing.*) Thankyou sir. Thankyou. Thank —

SKINNER. All right, all right.

CLOWN (*inspects the pistol*). Where d'you wind it up?

SKINNER. You don't wind it up! (*To the audience:*) Wind it up! (*Points at* FRED.) Hey take that man's gag out. Guess he's dyin t' laugh at our funny friend here.

STAGEHAND 3 *ungags* FRED. *The* STAGEHANDS *go, pointing to the* CLOWN, *making derisive gestures about him and miming laughs to each other.*

SKINNER. Don't blame you guys quittin while he's around.

FRED. Please. Please.

CLOWN. What a polite man!

SKINNER. Okay let's see you have first go.

CLOWN *aims at* SKINNER.

SKINNER. Other way! Other way!

CLOWN *aims at himself.*

SKINNER. O fine! Much better!

AUDIENCE. Lights! Lights! Lights!

SKINNER. My son's on the lights.

AUDIENCE *groans.*

SKINNER. All right Mrs Leggit Ralph'll fix it okay! (*He shouts off.*) How's things Ralph? Give us all there is.

The lights don't change.

FRED. I didn't do it. I didn't do it.

AUDIENCE. Why not? He's a pansy!

FRED. I keep tellin yer! Please!

AUDIENCE. Please!

SKINNER (*to* CLOWN). Look at the sights.

CLOWN (*running round stage*). Where? Where? Where?

SKINNER. On the end of your gun!

CLOWN. Sights? I thought you meant show-girls — an show-girls — an show-girls — an — (*Starts running round the stage again.*) Where? — where? — where — where? (*Stops. Raises his arm and aims the pistol at his armpit.*) If I press this little trigger fellas

do I get a little spray? (*The audience screams.*) Whassamatter
don't you want me to smell nice? (*Looks down the barrel.*)
Hello can Alice come out t' play with me — I mean play?
(*Puts the pistol to his ear.*) Huha operator. Huha. Huha. Huha
— (*Suddenly.*) O mother! I didn't recognize your voice. I
thought it was the answerin service. Yes mother. Yes mother.
(*Bored. Scratches his crutch and his behind with the pistol.
Quickly speaks into the phone.*) No mother I didn't say a word.
Must be a bad line. (*Smacks the pistol.*) You bad bad line.
Naughty.

FRED. Please!

AUDIENCE. Please!

FRED. I didn't. Didn't. Didn't. Didn't. I told yer. O please!
Please!

CLOWN. Is he tryin t' say somethin?

SKINNER. Look down the sights!

CLOWN (*running round the stage*). Show-girls — show-girls —
show-girls —

SKINNER. My last warnin!

CLOWN   *peers down the sights. He slowly leans forward till
he's almost horizontal.*

CLOWN. . . . . Show-girls . . . . show-girls . . . . show-girls —
show-girls — show-girls —

CLOWN *starts running round the stage again.*

SKINNER. That does it!

SKINNER *goes after the* CLOWN. CLOWN *rushes round the
stage. He gives the swing a push. It rises very high. The
audience screams and sings 'The Daring Young Man on the
Flying Trapeze!' CLOWN stares in fascination at the swing.
Tries to aim at it from the side. The swing keeps swinging out
of aim. CLOWN exasperated. Suddenly becomes very cunning.
Slowly creeps round to the front of the swing where it's easier
to aim.*

CLOWN (*foxy*). Ha-haaaaaa!

AUDIENCE. Ha-haaaaaaaaaaaaaaa!

CLOWN. One. Two.

FRED. O no!

CLOWN. Eleven. Eight. Seventy two. (*Counts fingers.*) Six.

FRED. Please.

CLOWN. What comes after six?

AUDIENCE. Three!

CLOWN. Can't hear!

AUDIENCE. Three!!

CLOWN (*to* FRED). What they say?

AUDIENCE. Three!!!

CLOWN. Seven!

> CLOWN *shoots* FRED — *with a jet of water. He squirts water under his arms. Under his crutch. Behind his ears. In his mouth. Gargles. Runs round stage shouting 'Show-girls'.* FRED *laughs with hysterical relief.*

FRED. O fellas. Fellas. I thought it was real. I thought you were goin — (*Laughing weakly.*) I thought it was real. I thought it was real.

CLOWN (*still running*). Where? Where? Where?

> CLOWN *pulls out the front of his trousers.*

CLOWN. Down boy! Down boy! Down! Down!

> CLOWN *squirts water into the front of his trousers. A stream comes back in retaliation. The audience roar.* SKINNER *pushes the swing to keep up momentum.* CLOWN *runs round the stage screaming with a hand over his eye.*

CLOWN. Blind! Blind! Blind! Blind! (*Shoots* FRED *in rage.* FRED *jerks violently. Screams.*) Foot!

AUDIENCE. Me! Me next! My turn!

> The first isolated shots escalate almost immediately into a disorderly volley.

> Knee! Foot! Arm! Leg! Gut! Chest! Head! Side! Front! Patsy! Dick!

SKINNER (*waving his arms from the side of the stage*). Order! Order!

> RALPH *rushes on, crouches at the side, shoots repeatedly.*

CLOWN *shoots once from the other side.*

AUDIENCE (*screams*). Lights! Lights! Lights! Lights! Lights!

FRED *spins, twists, jerks, screams. After screams, blood spurts. Lights snap to half, flicker out, come on immediately at full, fade, come back to full, cut out for a second, flash, come back to half, snap up to full.* RALPH *runs out, back, crouches, shoots.*

SKINNER. Hold it! Hold it! Hold it! Hold it!

Shooting stops. The audience noise seethes in a crescendo. SKINNER *runs to the swing, pushes it, runs back shaking blood from his hands.* RALPH *and* CLOWN *open fire.*

SKINNER. One more time!

Last volley. Audience noise explodes. FRED *has keeled over. He swings slowly and silently upside down. Blood falls and swishes over the stage.*

SKINNER. Hold it! Hold it!

SKINNER *marches authoritatively to the centre of the stage. He carries a hat. He holds it over his heart.*

SKINNER. Up! Up! Up!

SKINNER *starts to sing the American national anthem. The vaudeville orchestra joins in, in full, sonorous orchestration, and then the audience.* SKINNER *raises his hat and waves it like a venerable senator. The lights go. The music plays on.*

Scene Four

The same.

The music ends. The lights come up. It is morning. The body is still on the swing but a sheet has been thrown over it. A PHOTOGRAPHER *is crouching in front of it.* RALPH *and* STAGEHANDS 1 *and* 3 *watch.* STAGEHAND 2 *removes the cover. He pushes the swing once.* PAUL *comes through the audience and goes up on stage.*

PHOTOGRAPHER (*flash*). Fine. Fine. Dandy. Great.

The STAGEHANDS *start to take* FRED *down from the swing.* RALPH *supervises.*

RALPH (*sees* PAUL). Wait there Sambo.

PAUL *stands on the edge of the stage.*

STAGEHAND 1. We gonna paste him up outside town
Mr Skinner?

RALPH. Dad says.

STAGEHAND 1. On a tree?

RALPH (*nods*). Better git a box. He's a mess. Cartons outside.
We're movin goods in.

RALPH *goes out.* STAGEHAND 3 *helps the*
PHOTOGRAPHER: *he holds* FRED *in a sitting pose.*
STAGEHANDS 1 *and* 2 *watch.*

STAGEHAND 2. I was goin that way I'd expect more'n a poke off
off Miss Diary Kroll.

STAGEHAND 3. Heard she was so wide the doctor could've got
both arms in.

STAGEHAND 2. That where she keep her diary?

The STAGEHANDS *laugh.*

STAGEHAND 1. My kids told the wife she took t' goin down the
river. Make out she's took short. Hitch up her skirt an squat.
(*Flash.*) The long yeller grass tickle her tail. (STAGEHANDS
laugh.) Regular habit.

RALPH *comes back.*

STAGEHAND 1. Kids got t' know. Followed her down. I clip
their ears. Know what they get up to down there.

RALPH *carries a large cardboard carton. It's taller than it's
long. Stencilled on its side in black is a brand sign and the
number and weight of the tins it contained. The*
STAGEHANDS *start to lift* FRED *into the carton.* RALPH
goes to PAUL.

RALPH. Where was you?

PAUL. Come for my things.

RALPH. Your job was on lights. That's disobeyin orders.

STAGEHAND 2. Shoe catchin.

PHOTOGRAPHER. Hold it. (*Flash.*)

RALPH. Don't disobey orders.

STAGEHAND 1. 'S luck have it he set double.

RALPH. Orders is good for the health.

RALPH goes back to the others. PAUL goes off into the wings.

PHOTOGRAPHER. I do two regular sizes. Twelve by eight for mountin an wallet size t' carry round an show folks. I'll send a list round. You fill in your name an requirements.

RALPH. Okay.

The STAGEHANDS drop the sheet into the top of the carton.

PHOTOGRAPHER. Sorry — cash in advance.

RALPH. Okay.

PAUL comes on stage. He carries a medium size suitcase. He walks over the stage.

PHOTOGRAPHER. Been caught too often. Weddin's. Sunday school outin's. Masonics. You'd be surprised.

PAUL. Okay, okay.

MRS KROLL comes on.

MRS KROLL. Paul your case . . .

The STAGEHANDS lift the carton by the bottom corners. They carry it out slowly and carefully.

PAUL (*stops*). I quit Mrs Kroll.

MRS KROLL. Paul!

RALPH. You makin some sort of protest over last night?

PAUL. Applied for my job a month back. Check with the mine office.

MRS KROLL. Greta's ill. I can't cope. She knows you.

PAUL (*refusing*). Sorry.

MRS KROLL (*crying*). It's too bad. On top of everything.

RALPH (*goes to her*). Mrs Kroll you can't cry for a nigger. (*Puts his arm round her shoulder.*) That's gonna upset folks. You can't cope with Miss Kroll? She'll go in a good institution. The best. I'm sure folks of this town'd git up a subscription. Why I guess the Justice Riders'd start it off with part of last night's proceeds. They always support a good cause.

The STAGEHANDS wander back. STAGEHAND 3 has a bottle of beer. They watch RALPH take MRS KROLL out.

STAGEHAND. Mrs Kroll sure is sore at you.

STAGEHAND 3 sits on the swing. He opens the bottle and drinks.

STAGEHAND 1 (*little laugh. Nods at the swing*). Mostly *black* folk die so spectacular.

STAGEHAND 3 (*giggles*). One time you could've stayed for the fun Paul. (*Stands suddenly.*) Have a peep!

STAGEHAND 2. No sir! That make Paul nervous!

The STAGEHANDS laugh quietly and easily for a moment. PAUL drops a dime on the stage. The STAGEHANDS laugh and scramble for it.

STAGEHAND 2 (*laughing*). Mine!

STAGEHAND 3 (*laughing*). Get off!

STAGEHAND 1 (*laughing*). Got it first!

STAGEHAND 2 (*laughing*). Will you shove off!

The STAGEHANDS scrap playfully for the coin. They laugh and mug each other a little.

STAGEHAND 3 (*rolling on the ground*). I got Paul's dime! Hey Paul why you throw your dime away?

STAGEHAND 2. Paul always was a show off.

STAGEHAND 3. Bye Paul. Keep good!

STAGEHAND 2 has knocked the dime from STAGEHAND 3's hand. They roll, cuff, laugh, and ruffle each other's hair. In the fight the swing is knocked. It zooms from side to side — not in the direction of the normal swing — over their rolling bodies. PAUL has gone.

STAGEHAND 1. It's mine anyway!

They giggle and tussle. They get up, snatch at each other and wander away.

Stone

A short play

Stone

Men are not asked who they are but ordered to be
Cut to the shape of a square world
And the head bound as surely as Old China
Bound women's feet

Why this unreason?
The tool-user makes tools for his purpose
They work? — no questions!
They break? — new ones!

Just make enough noise to drown your voice
Turn on enough light to blind you
Block out the windows with light
Run long enough to learn how to sleep on the run
This is the first obligation on all tools:
Don't know your own function

So what weight presses you to the ground?
Why does the young hand shake with the palsy of age?

What is the definition of a tool?
A space that exactly fills its prison

Author's Note

The author wrote *Stone* when Gay Sweatshop asked him for a play. He wrote the following programme note for the first production.

To support an injustice to anyone else damages your own life. It involves you in physical repression and violence which can in extreme cases cost you your life (in wars, in hooliganism created by urban decay, in racial violence, and so on). It also involves you in mental and emotional distortions. To justify injustice reality is replaced with myths — for example, that people are born evil, blacks are bad, the tory party is the party of born leaders, strikers want to smash the country. This distortion trivializes human relationships; and as it prevents the rational solution of problems, it produces hysteria and violence.
All major repressions — Nazi anti-semitism, black slavery, the persecution of homosexuals — are signs of the injustice of the whole of the society in which they occur.
  Most societies are led by those who profit from injustice. There is a vested interest in injustice (and therefore in irrationality). So, it used to be said that male homosexuals were effeminate and this endangered the empire. No emancipation for homosexuals was possible until imperialism began to crack. Anyone fighting for the freedom and self-respect of colonialised Africans and Asians — or, for that matter, of colonialised factory workers in Europe — is fighting for the freedom and self-respect of homosexuals everywhere; anyone fighting *against* colonial freedom and the emancipation of the working class is just as surely fighting for the repression of homosexuals. To give another example: until more money and effort are spent on a good, universal education for all children — without a money-right to opt into privileged elites — then (at the poor end of

society) city roughs will go on queer-bashing sprees, and (at the rich end) public schools will teach scorn and fear of homosexuality. Privilege creates violence as much as deprivation.

You cannot have your freedom at anyone else's expense. Freedom is indivisible. From time to time the struggle for it is waged on different fronts, on those where the next victories seem most possible or most needed. But the struggle is a general one. Homosexual emancipation is not possible without economic and political reforms in other parts of society: in schools, factories, hospitals, legislatures. Unless they support these reforms homosexuals are aiding in their own repression.

I believe it was Einstein who said a society's level of civilization could be judged by its attitude to anti-semitism. Later this was said about capital punishment. We could now say it about homosexuality — except that there are so many things it could also be said about.

Stone was first presented by Gay Sweatshop at the I.C.A. Theatre, London, on 8 June 1976. The cast was as follow:

MAN	Kevin Elyot
MASON/JUDGE	Tony Douse
TRAMP/POLICEMAN/BOY	Antony Sher
GIRL/WASHERWOMAN	Anna Nygh

Directed by Gerald Chapman
Designed by Mary Moore
Music by Robert Campbell
Choreography by Liebe Klug

Scene One

Road. Empty stage. A young MAN *comes on. He is eager and relaxed. A middle-aged man comes on. He is quiet and efficient and wears a business suit. He is a* MASON.

MASON. Where are you off to?

MAN (*half smiles*). Why?

MASON. You're not lost?

MAN. No, I'm going to find a job and make my place in the world.

MASON. Good luck.

MAN. Thanks. (*Smiles.*) I left home this morning. My father and mother can't keep me now.

MASON. What work d'you want?

MAN. I could learn to do almost anything.

MASON. What did your parents give you to take out in the world?

MAN (*touches his pocket. Half smiles*). Something.

MASON. Generous!

MAN. They didn't have much but they wouldn't let me go empty handed.

MASON. How much?

MAN (*cunning*). Ha-ha.

MASON. Do I look like a thief?

MAN. You might be a clever thief.

MASON. I'm weaker than you. You could knock me down.

MAN. That's true.

MASON. But you wouldn't.

MAN. Why not?

MASON. I'm very rich. But I don't carry money on me. So I

agree: it's not worth knocking me down. Congratulations on changing your mind.

MAN. I didn't change my mind! I never meant to knock you down.

MASON. No? You'll find — out in the world — it's better to expect the worst. (*Takes out a pistol.*) Like this.

MAN (*shortly*). O.

MASON. How much?

MAN. Not much.

MASON. How much?

MAN. Seven gold talents.

MASON (*blandly*). Seven. (*Jerks the pistol.*) Show me.

The MAN *takes out seven gold coins.*

MASON. Pockets out.

The MAN *pulls out his pockets. They are empty.*

MASON. Hand it over. (*He names each coin as it is put into his hands.*) Prudence, soberness, courage, justice, honesty, love — (*The* MAN *drops a coin.*) Pick it up. (*The* MAN *picks it up and gives it to the* MASON.) Hope. Now what will you do?

MAN. I won't go home.

MASON. They can't afford to take you back.

MAN. I'd be ashamed to ask them. I wasted their money. They worked so hard for it.

MASON. They should have warned you about thieves.

MAN. They did. But the sun was shining and I thought no one would spoil a day like this by stealing. I shall go to the police.

MASON. Then I shall have to shoot you. You're spoiling my day too!

MAN (*annoyed with himself*). Blast.

MASON. You'll really have to control your tongue. (*Sighs. Shakes his head.*) Shooting people works out expensive. Fortunately I don't have to shoot you. The police are far too busy to worry about your seven talents!

MASON *gives the money back to the* MAN.

MAN. O. (*Puts the money in his pocket grumpily.*) Thanks.

MASON. Let me give you a job.

MAN. Don't pull my leg.

MASON. What?

MAN. You won't give me a job.

MASON. Why not?

MAN. You wouldn't trust me. You made me look a fool. I didn't show much sense did I?

MASON (*nodding*). Yes, you'll suit me very well.

MAN. It must be such hard work you can't get anyone else to do it.

MASON. No, it's the sort of job people queue up for.

MAN. What's the catch?

MASON. Can't someone just want to help you?

MAN. No.

MASON. Your parents did.

MAN. That's different.

MASON. You bring out my paternal instinct.

MAN. What job is it?

MASON (*takes a stone from his pocket*). Here's a stone. No more than a pebble really. Take it to my house.

MAN. That stone?

MASON. My house is along the road.

MAN. Why don't you take it?

MASON. My business takes me the other way.

MAN. Let me look. (*The* MASON *holds the stone on the flat of his palm.*) Is it an ordinary stone?

MASON. It's just as you see it.

MAN. Why d'you want it?

MASON. I'm a stone mason. No doubt I see more in it than you do.

MAN (*takes the stone*). It looks ordinary.

MASON. I told you.

MAN. How far is your house?

MASON. Quite a way. You'll come to it. Tell them I sent you.

MAN. Why an ordinary stone?

MASON. It could be the ordinariness that interests me.

MAN. And wages?

MASON. You're paid when you deliver the goods.

MAN. How much?

MASON. That depends how quickly you deliver them.

MAN (*returns the stone*). That's the catch.

MASON (*shrugs*). I don't pay in advance.

MAN. I don't work till I'm paid.

MASON. You won't find an easier job.

MAN. I don't trust you.

MASON. I want to help you. But I won't give money away. That ruins people, especially the young. Encourages scrounging. Deliver this stone — that's not much to ask. I could have robbed you. Instead I offer you an easy job — and you say you don't trust me! I'll be on my way. (*Starts to go.*)

MAN. Well — (*Stops short.*)

MASON (*turning round*). Yes?

MAN. How will I know your house?

MASON. It's by a stone-yard.

MAN. Suppose someone offers me a better job?

MASON. They'll offer to carry *you*?

MAN. I might get lost or fed up.

MASON. Now you see the place of trust. I have to trust you. You could throw my stone away anytime. But I trust you. Within reason. That's why I don't pay till you deliver the goods.

MAN. I see.

MASON. And you have to trust me. Within reason. I say wait to be paid — but I ask so little. If I'd said murder your grandmother — I'd have asked too much. You'd expect to be paid first. Rightly. Or if I'd said sell your soul. Kill your brothers. Swallow the ocean. Then you wouldn't want to be paid at all! — because you're a good lad and you'd rather live by your talents. While they last. So I ask little: carry a stone. And I only ask that because it's the easiest way I can help you without offending my principles. It would be very odd if you said no.

MAN. Yes, I see.

MASON. So you enter my employ?

MAN. Er yes.

MASON (*raised finger*). Call me sir now you're one of mine.

MAN. Yes sir.

MASON (*gives the stone to the* MAN). Excellent.

MAN. I'll take it to your house as quickly as I can.

MASON. Mind you do boy. Good day.

MAN. Yes sir.

> *The* MASON *goes out.*

MAN. As he said: if I get tired or find something better I can throw it away. It can't do any harm till then.

David and Goliath, or Song of False Optimism

Goliath was bigger than a mountain
David killed him with a stone
Goliath fell down like a landslide
David was light on his feet
He saw the shadow fall over him
And stepped aside just in time

David knelt to thank the lord
Goliath in the kicks of death
Raised his fist — it came down like a bomb
David had good hearing
He heard the mighty rushing of wind
And stepped aside just in time

David sang a victory song
Out of the hole in Goliath's head
An evil gas poured over the world
David had a good sense of smell
He smelt the air turning septic
And got out of that just in time

David danced a dance of praise
When Goliath was struck his spear had spun
High in the air — it came down like a bomb
David had a good sense of touch
He felt the tip scratch the top of his skull
And stepped aside just in time

The MAN *goes.*

Scene Two

Road. Empty stage. An Irish TRAMP *comes on. He is ill, shivering and exhausted. He mutters darkly to himself.*

TRAMP. God damn and blast this blidy earth . . . the creatures in it . . . and the sky that covers it. (*Takes out a bottle. Swigs.*) Ah. (*The 'ah' is perfunctorily routine.*) Curse the day he made it. (*Sits on the ground and weeps quietly.*) Was he like a man tryin on a pair of new shoes? (*Small swig.*) 'I'll try them for size. Hang on now, it don't fit. Pinches me toe. Don't think much of the colour of the welt. Have you anthin more in the fashion?' Tosses us aside in the dark and we've been festerin on a dump site ever since. (*Examines his shoe. Flaps the sole.*) Piss swamp. I was a scholar. We had books in the family. I've been drunk so many years I don't know if I've forgotten how to read or I just see the words double.

The MAN *comes in. He is tired. The* TRAMP *hides his bottle.*

MAN. Are you all right?

TRAMP. Do I look all right?

MAN. No.

TRAMP. At least one of us sees straight.

MAN. What's the matter?

TRAMP. I have this terrible pain.

MAN. Where?

TRAMP. All over. Have you anythin to drink?

MAN. No.

TRAMP. Or eat? (*The* MAN *shakes his head.*) Well don't stand there! I'm not a blidy peep-show.

MAN. I wanted to help.

TRAMP. You're a decent lad. Sorry. I suppose you haven't any money?

MAN. A bit.

TRAMP. Ouch. O dear. What a terrible stab of pain.

MAN. Where?

TRAMP. I wouldn't have believed it could have got that worse if me mother had swore it on the day she died with one hand on the bible and the other on me father's grave — I'm an orphan you understand.

MAN. I'm sorry.

TRAMP. A sorrow shared is a sorrow halved. Give us a hand now.

MAN. Right. (*Helps the* TRAMP *to stand.*)

TRAMP. Fine, fine. (*On his feet.*) Let go and watch. (MAN *lets him go. He staggers.*) There now, see that? Brain damage.

MAN. How?

TRAMP. Will you stop interruptin. These are probably the last words of a dyin man — it'd be a mortal sin if you stopped me gettin me message to the world. I'll sit down and save strength. (*Sits.*) You were sent to me by god. I bet you didn't know that.

MAN. No.

TRAMP. Ho-ho god moves in a mysterious way. He's called people far worse than yourself. O dear here comes the pain again — not that it went away. I'll take a drop of this to keep me goin till me mortal work is done. (*Swigs.*) Now what would your job be? Don't tell me, let me guess. A clever lad like you, you'll be in a well-paid line of trade. You're a doctor.

MAN (*smiles*). No!

TRAMP. You're not? I could have sworn. *Now* I have you! A fine lookin lad like you — you're an actor.

MAN. No.

TRAMP. This is difficult. Good with your hands I bet. I have it, I have it, I have it! Civil Engineer.

MAN. No.

TRAMP. You play the violin.

MAN. No.

TRAMP. Then I'm beat. I'm afraid you'll have to tell me how you earned your money.

MAN. I didn't.

TRAMP. The man's a riddle.

MAN. My parents gave it to me.

TRAMP. He's a blidy heir!

MAN. No — I've just come out in the world.

TRAMP. Well where the blidy hell had you been before? A joke! O it takes me back. Many years ago — not all that many — I was just as strong and handsome as yourself. To look at you I'd say you came from a good family, but — don't be offended, in my eyes it's a compliment — poor.

MAN. That's right.

TRAMP. I could see there was no taint of luxury in you. (*Sighs.*) If they were poor they couldn't have give you much. No, I won't be told! I'll guess. Jassus-christ if I don't guess somethin right I'll lose me self-respect. You don't want that! Half a talent.

MAN. No.

TRAMP. Never a whole talent?

MAN. No.

TRAMP. It couldn't be more? I don't believe it. A talent and a half?

MAN. No.

TRAMP. Och you're talkin of copper. That could never be gold.

MAN. Gold.

TRAMP. Glory be! What a wonderful upbringin you'd get from

people like that. You must have the manners of a saint. So it's
three talents!

MAN. No.

TRAMP. Tch tch tch, to think of them poor people slavin
away for the sake of their lad. Four?

MAN. No.

TRAMP. Wearin their fingers to the bone. Their hair turnin
grey before its time. All so they could see their lad go out and
make the world a better place. (*Sighs.*) You'll have to tell me
son. Sorry to let you down but with parents like that how
could I tell what they'd do? I see the world's not all bad. I'll
die happy with the amount of their goodness ringin in my
ears. How much was it — the excitement's killin me.

MAN. Seven.

TRAMP (*swigs*). I don't believe that.

MAN. It's true.

TRAMP. It's blidy not. Was I born yesterday? Aren't you
ashamed, lyin and blackguardin your family's name after all
they've done for you?

The MAN *takes out the seven coins.*

TRAMP. Glory be. The fella's a walkin miracle. And there's me
callin him scoundrel.

MAN (*showing the coins*). Prudence, soberness, courage, justice,
honesty, love —

He drops a coin. The TRAMP *picks it up.*

TRAMP (*reads the coin*). Hope. Glory be. Before I hand this coin
back I'll tell you a story. It has a moral and it's true. Twenty
years ago I stepped into the world just like yourself, smilin
and bellowin top of the mornin till people thought I was
mad. And now? (*Sighs.*) How did I get this way you ask? One
mornin an old fella came towards me on this road, on this
very spot — for I've gone round in circles ever since. He was
dirty and stinkin and broken. He held out his hand — so.
Nothing was said. I had gold — it chinked in my pocket as I
crossed over and passed by. I wasn't rich like you — me
mother was a widow — but I had enough t' make me hard.
That night I sat under a hedge and counted me coins. Every

night I ran them through me fingers. This night, back of the hedge — robbers. Out they hops. Thwack the head-lad thumps me cross the head with his stick. Me brain was damaged. And I've been the wreck you see ever since. (*Flips the coin and catches it.*) Now if I'd given me money to the old fella I'd be a man still — and richer than I was then. I had a dream. The lord sent you. Let me save your soul. (*Holds out his hand.*)

The MAN *drops another coin in the* TRAMP's *hand, walks away, and turns round to face him.*

MAN. I don't believe a word.

TRAMP. Hahaa—hahaa, the lord says it doesn't matter if it never happened to me! It could happen to you.

MAN. I'll have to take my chance like anyone else.

TRAMP (*lies on the ground and cries*). I let that poor fella die on the road. Now I'm losing this young one. How can I save his soul? It's terrible!

MAN. You've got two coins. No more.

TRAMP (*howls*). How can I make him see? How? (*Beats the ground in despair.*) I'm not after your money! (*Kneels and clasps hands in prayer.*) God inspire me! Don't let me lose another sheep! (*Sudden inspiration.*) Ah! Yes! Thankyou god. (*Turns solemnly to face the* MAN. *Slowly takes a knife from inside his coat. Holds it out.*)

MAN. I'll kill you first.

The MAN *takes the stone from his pocket. It is recognisably the same stone but it has grown to the size of a brick.*

TRAMP. God didn't say I was to kill you. He said I was to kill meself. (*He holds the point of the knife against his own throat.*)

MAN. You won't.

TRAMP. Ah I will. What d'you know of me? I sleep in the road. Filthy, stinkin, drunk, out all weathers. Two talents — I'll drink it away! I'd be better off with nothin. Seven talents — I could start again. Get warm and clean and decent. Find a dry place to live. (*Jerks dagger at his throat.*) I'm on me last legs. You're young. Your life's to come. Why did your people give you money? To grow fat? Or make the world — god forgive me for a blasphemous| swine for saying so — a better

place? (*Throws the two coins on the ground, but not too far.*)
There's your money with the blood on it!

MAN. You won't.

TRAMP. You haven't seen your man die yet. You think they only
stink when they're dead. No, dyin has its own smell. An
acidy stink — suddenly in the air — worse than decay. And its
sounds. You never hear them somewhere else. Heels drummin
as if you're marching downhill. A matchbox rattlin in the
throat. O not loud. You could still sip your tea through it if
you'd been well brought up. The sound furniture makes in a
doll's house when children are playin. Nothin matters more
than a game, and nothin's more quickly forgotten when it's
over. That's life my boyo! My death will be the end of the
game. Watch me play! Snip you're dead!

The MAN *comes back to the* TRAMP. *Suddenly he dives for
the coins. The* TRAMP *moves violently — still with the knife at
at his throat. They each get one.*

MAN. I'll buy the knife.

TRAMP. Seven talents.

MAN (*drops a coin*). Two.

TRAMP. Seven. Hurry. It's nearly time, the whistle'll blow.

MAN. Three. No more.

TRAMP. Four more. Four! By god this is a moment I'd choose to
die in! All or nothin! The lot staked! Seven. Coin of the
realm.

MAN (*drops four more coins*). That's all. I shall hold on to this
one.

TRAMP. Yes . . . well . . . six. But I've been cheated. (*Bites a
coin.*) It it good money? Yes, gold — you swindler . . .

MAN. Give me the knife.

TRAMP. That cost *seven* talents! O I won't pig-stick meself. The
knife act is over, the cabaret's finished. I'll take me death off
your conscience for six talents. But I'll keep the knife. One
day you might get it in the back.

They start to go in opposite directions.

MAN (*out front*). Every evening I measure this stone and it's bigger. The mason is up to something. Something good will happen to me when I deliver it. Some special reward. (*Looks at his coin.*) Hope. I'm glad I gave the rest of my money to him. My kindness will make the world a better place. I'll cling to my stone! The world is full of surprises.

Merlin and Arthur

Merlin was a great wizard
He took eggs from the air
He took a loaf from a beggar's sleeve
He even made a corpse smile
By letting it smell his fingers

TRAMP (*out front. Counts the coins*). Glory be. (*Shakes his head.*) The man's dangerous. He shouldn't be allowed out on the road.

King Arthur was a jealous king
He took the loaf and eggs
The dead man had been his worst enemy
He'd killed him in battle
So he hanged Merlin for treason.

Scene Three

An Inn. Empty stage — perhaps an inn sign. GIRL *enters.*

GIRL. This inn's called 'The Dance of the Seven Deadly Veils'. I run it on my own. Not easy! I ought to marry. There's a lot of men I'd like to share my bed — no problem, as long as they know a thing or two — but no one I'd like to share my profits — the problem there is they know too much! There's a lot of men I'd trust with another woman — frankly I'm not bothered! — but no one I'd trust with my till! I've got a good business. Customers come miles to see my famous dance. But I could do better. A weak woman gets put upon.

Song of the Seven Deadly Veils

How is society organised?
For the happiness of the people?
Or so that profit can be drawn
At as many points as possible?
What do you want from the cow?

Milk or blood?
Then stop sticking your knife in
All over its hide

The governor begging at the widow's door
The soldier as protector of the poor
The strongman waiting humbly for the weak
The spokesman who gives up his turn to speak
When things like this are seen
The world will be a better place
Than it has been

> Evil creates its own remedy!
> Till then we stagger round and lose our breath
> In that old Side Show called The Dance of Death

> In the famous dance of the seven deadly veils
> Bad turns to good
> Homes turn to jails
> Can turns to should
> A corkscrew is straight
> Saints turn to whores
> But don't send to ask who's head is on the plate:
> It's yours!

The priest and teacher whisper together
Mankind is a tragic animal
Destined by nature to fight forever
Man against man with tooth and claw
But our pyramids!
Will this brawling pack ever get them built?
Call in the overseer!

The workingman who gets some time for thought
The thinker who's conclusions can't be bought
The office-seeker who can use a spade
The specialist who cures before he's paid
When things like this are seen
The world will be a better place
Than it has been

> Evil creates its own remedy!
> Till then we stagger round and lose our breath
> In that old Side Show called The Dance of Death

> In the famous dance of the seven deadly veils
> Bad turns to good

Homes turn to jails
Can turns to should
A corkscrew is straight
Saints turn to whores
But don't send to ask whose head is on the plate:
It's yours!

All men must work or scheme to get money
To buy food and shelter for their families
The Greatest Profit is king of this jungle
That's how vices become virtues!
What follows?
When the judge's throat is cut
It's done by his own law!

The scientist who builds his life on truth
The judge who convicts only after proof
The son who never bore his father's curse
The king who doesn't ride behind a hearse.
When things like this are seen
The world will be a better place
Than it has been

Evil creates its own remedy!
Till then we stagger round and lose our breath
In that old Side Show called The Dance of Death

In the famous dance of the seven deadly veils
Bad turns to good
Homes turn to jails
Can turns to should
A corkscrew is straight
Saints turn to whores
But don't send to ask whose head is on the plate:
It's yours!

The MAN *enters. He is much older — tired, filthy and
exhausted. The stone has become a large rock. He carries it on
his shoulders. It doubles him up and makes him stagger.*

MAN. Let me stay at your inn.

GIRL. Any money?

MAN. No.

GIRL. Move on.

MAN. A cup of water.

GIRL. What're you carrying?

MAN. Give me some bread.

GIRL. What's that?

MAN. A stone.

GIRL. Where're you taking it?

MAN. The stone mason's house.

GIRL. How much does he pay you?

MAN. I won't know till I get there.

GIRL. Have you carried it far?

MAN. O yes. I keep asking people where he lives and they just
point on and say further. I'm tired and hungry and cold and
the stone gets heavier everyday. But I can't give up now. All
my sufferings would be wasted.

GIRL. Put it down.

MAN. No! This is a pub. People keep coming and going. It might
be stolen. (*Groans*.) The nights are terrible! Once I could sleep
with it on my chest. Now I have to lie on it.

GIRL. What loyalty! (*Aside*.) This is the idiot I'm looking for.
Carried that all this way for nothing! — He won't have his
hand in the till the moment my back's turned. (*To the* MAN:)
Put it down. It's all right, it's gone closing time.

MAN. Thank you.

The GIRL *helps him to put the stone on the ground. He sits on
it and sings.*

The Cliffs, or Bad Dream

The white cliffs that stand by the sea
Every night the black water stirs itself
And leaves its bed
And seizes the cliffs
And takes them down to a hole
Under the sea
And in the dark like a blind torturer
It tortures them with pain and supplice
And before there is light it sends them back
To the edge of the sea

And they stand and stare at the black water
Stirring listlessly in its sleep
All day

GIRL. The mason used to be my customer. He's dead. Sorry to
bring bad news.

MAN. What shall I do? He can't be dead!

GIRL. We need disaster to kick us up the arse now and then or
we'd never move. You know what they say, a diamond's only
granite that's had more to bear. I need a chucker out. There's
a man in the back — he's been boozing and stuffing for twelve
months! Make him cough up and chuck him out. Then you can
wash the dishes. The roof needs mending. And the garden
wouldn't know what a spade was if it saw one. A few rows of
peas and potatoes. I've nothing against home-grown produce.
You get one good meal a day and your drink — but I limit the
drink, publicans should abstain. And you can watch me
dance — you'd never afford the prices! (*Feels his arm.*) Right
little porter. Feed you up and who knows, I could be very
friendly. (*Calls.*) Pig! Out! The trotter man's here! (*Off,
grunting and grumbling.*) Hear it? (*Calls.*) Pig, the pork
butcher's come with his knife!

TRAMP (*off*). Who's blidy drunk my drink while I was asleep?

Noises. The TRAMP *comes on.*

TRAMP. Who're you callin pig you blidy sow? This blidy run-
down sty! Give us a drink. (*Sees the* MAN.) Who — (*Recognises
him.*) Ho ho. The late Mr Money! Are you sniffin round that
she-animal? She only does it for money and believe me laddie
you'd get better satisfaction puttin your little penny in the
slot of a china piggy bank.

GIRL (*gives the* TRAMP *a bill*). Six month's lodgings and good
living. Pay up.

TRAMP. No!

GIRL (*to the* MAN:) Do him.

TRAMP. Mr Rockerfella? He won't throw his pal out on the
streets! He'd step aside to let a fly pass.

GIRL. Then he won't stand idle while I'm robbed. (*Shows her
wrist to the* MAN.) See that mark? Him, the swine.

TRAMP. The only way to get sense into her is hammer it in.

The MAN *hits him.*

TRAMP (*blinks. Turns to the* GIRL). Has your booze suddenly got better or did he hit me?

The MAN *hits him. The* TRAMP *takes out his knife.*

TRAMP (*through his teeth*): You little swine now.

A fight. They roll on the floor. The TRAMP *flails with the knife. They go into a clinch. The* MAN *tries to break the* TRAMP's *neck by forcing his chin back. The* GIRL *speaks in the silence.*

GIRL. You say do as you would be done by
But you don't know what you do
So you do as you are done by
That's all you are able to do

The TRAMP *bites the man. The* MAN *gouges the* TRAMP's *eyes. They both dive for the knife. The* TRAMP *gets it. He lashes out. The knife sticks in the floor. The* MAN *knocks the* TRAMP *out. The* TRAMP *is still. The* MAN *doubles over gasping for breath. He rips open the* TRAMP's *pockets. He takes out the coins.*

GIRL. At last! Money.

MAN (*turns away gasping*). Mine.

GIRL. . . . All right lovie. Lug him out the back. I'll see you're all right.

The MAN, *still gasping for breath, drags out the* TRAMP. *The* GIRL *prepares for the dance. She brings food, drink, a pillow and seven white sheets. She goes out again. The* MAN *returns.*

MAN (*counting his money*). One, two . . . . six. (*He takes the coin from his pocket.*) Seven. (*He sees the food and goes to it.*)

GIRL (*off, harshly*): Wait!

MAN. I'll pay for —

GIRL (*off, harshly*): Sit!

The MAN *sits. The* GIRL *comes on naked.*

GIRL. This is my famous dance of the seven deadly veils.

INSTRUCTIONS FOR THE DANCE:

The GIRL *begins by dancing wildly. She stops seven times. Each time she stops she asks the* MAN *for a coin, he gives it to*

*her, and she covers herself with a white sheet. Each time she
dances a little more slowly. After the first coin she gives the
MAN the food and drink and the pillow to sit on. After each
coin he eats and drinks a little more slowly. The dance ends
with the MAN crawling back to his stone to sleep and the
GIRL stumbling to a standstill. She is shrouded from head to
foot and cries quietly under her shrouds. These are the lines
she uses to ask for the seven coins:*

First coin for the meat.
Second coin for the plate.
Third coin for the wine.
Fourth coin for the cup.
Fifth coin for the bread.
Sixth coin for the roof over your head.
Seventh coin for the dance.

MAN. Okay grub. Didn't think much of the dance.

GIRL (*crying quietly*). So naked. So naked. Cover me.

The MAN has gone to sleep. A POLICEMAN enters.

POLICEMAN. What's going on then? (*Sees the GIRL.*)
Disgusting! (*Slaps her face under the shrouds. She starts to
come round. He kicks the MAN.*) Don't sit on the ground, it's
an offence to drop litter.

MAN (*wakes*). What?

POLICEMAN. No doubt you've had a nasty dream so you won't
be at all surprised when I tell you there's a corpse on the front
doorstep and I'm arresting you for murder.

MAN. I didn't do it!

POLICEMAN (*picks up the knife*). Doesn't look like it. (*To the
GIRL:*) I arrest you for performing in an indecent show.

GIRL. I'm an artist!

POLICEMAN. Twist the judge's balls and he may believe you.
(*Points to the props.*) Pick them up.

*The MAN and the GIRL collect the props. The MAN carries
the stone and the GIRL the other things. They leave with the
POLICEMAN.*

Scene Four

Court. The JUDGE *brings his chair on. Sits. The* POLICEMAN *comes on.*

JUDGE. Let's start.

POLICEMAN (*calls off*). This way!

> *The* MAN *and the* GIRL *come in. The* MAN *is without the stone.*

GIRL (*recognizes the* JUDGE). My landlord.

POLICEMAN. Silence!

JUDGE. Another word and I'll charge you with contempt. Constable?

POLICEMAN. I was proceeding down Bartholomew Street in the course of my duty when I chanced upon a male figure alyin recumbent in the gutter. I disturbed it with my toe but achieved no response. I noticed that it had a three-day's growth of beard and concluded it was an Irishman. I took the fact that it was in the gutter at eleven in the forenoon as corroboratory evidence. Naturally, therefore, the man was drunk or asleep or both. Having already elicited no response with the end of my toe — the little one, sir — I concluded he was asleep. I thereupon lent forward to examine the breath. Imagine the surprise with which I discovered that although a stale smell of beer did indeed linger round his mouth it was — if I may use the image — a smell such as you get outside the door of a pub when it's locked at closing time. I.e. the man was dead. He lay outside a house of ill-repute —

GIRL. I object —

POLICEMAN. — known as 'The Inn of the Seven Deadly Veils', which establishment I've long had my eye on. I entered. I found the female accused in the last stages of a most lascivious performance —

GIRL. Liar!

POLICEMAN. — which, I see from her statement, she calls a dance.

GIRL. I'm an artist!

POLICEMAN. The male accused was recumbent upon the floor in a lethargic condition. I concluded this was the result of him just having finished killing the body on the doorstep.

GIRL. I demand a retrial!

JUDGE. The inn in question is an old established business. The account books show that all taxes, dues and rents are paid up to date. We've had no complaints in the past — not to speak of. I conclude — without at all doubting your word officer —

POLICEMAN. Thankyou sir.

JUDGE. — or the obscenity it was your misfortune to observe —

POLICEMAN. That night when I looked down at the curly heads of my little tots sleeping so innocently in their beds I was overwhelmed with fury that these things can be.

JUDGE. — that we may nevertheless not yet have the whole story. Madam, this court offers you its protection. Any threats that have been made to you can be dealt with. Help the court!

GIRL. Ah your honour. Well. That man — I should say monster — broke into my home, killed my best friend — just after he'd asked for my hand in marriage and offered me his protection in business affairs (the damages are going to be enormous!) — stole food and drink and forced me to perform a disgusting obscenity the memory of which will make me blush with shame to the roots of my hair even when as a result of this it goes prematurely grey.

JUDGE. Tch tch. (*To the* MAN:) I presume you throw yourself on the mercy of the court?

MAN. I didn't do it! I hit him but not that hard! I'm a respectable citizen.

JUDGE. Look at your clothes.

MAN. I got like this carrying a stone.

JUDGE. What stone?

MAN. A man asked me to carry it.

JUDGE. Why?

MAN. I don't know.

JUDGE. But you said yes?

MAN. It was a small stone then. It grew.

JUDGE. Don't feign madness here.

MAN. It grew!

JUDGE. If you're resolved to fritter away the court's goodwill on —

MAN. I paid for what I got. With good money. She's still got it.

JUDGE. Madam?

GIRL. Well.

JUDGE. Am I to be disappointed in everyone? Constable!

The POLICEMAN *takes the seven coins from the* GIRL.

JUDGE. Is this your money?

MAN. Yes.

JUDGE. What's their value Constable?

POLICEMAN (*reads the coins*): Pride. Greed. Lust. Envy —

MAN. That's not my money!

JUDGE. You said it was!

POLICEMAN (*reads*): Gluttony. Anger. Sloth.

GIRL. No wonder he smiled when he paid. He's a swindler! Paying with bad coin!

MAN. It's changed.

JUDGE. And the stone grew and the Irishman died of cold.

MAN (*points to the* POLICEMAN). He did it! He must have! He thought he was drunk. Gave him a kick — with his little toe! — and killed him! I'm taking the rap!

JUDGE. Tch tch.

POLICEMAN. Do I have to answer the wild accusations flung at my head sir?

JUDGE. I think you should. This is a court of justice before it's a court of law. The accused is allowed his say. Of course you may preserve a dignified — under the circumstances, even pained — silence and allow the court to draw a conclusion based on the contrast between your calm stoical demeanour and the violent hysteria of the accused and the coincidence that blue is its favourite colour.

MAN. He killed him!

POLICEMAN. I elect to defend myself because I consider it the duty of every good citizen to co-operate fully with the police which happens to be myself.

JUDGE. If only more thought so.

POLICEMAN. I've been kicking people all my life. I've kicked them in all postures from every conceivable angle at every time of the day and night in all seasons of the year. I'm a skilled kicker by profession and a cognoscente of kicking by inclination. I think I may say — with my reputation for expert kicking hanging in the balance — that my kick is controlled. Now if the accused is suggesting that I kicked a man and accidentally killed him, that suggestion is palpably ludicrous.

MAN. He killed him on purpose!

JUDGE. Pride, greed, lust, envy, gluttony, anger, sloth.

MAN. I'm not a murderer!

JUDGE. Constable?

POLICEMAN. I'm not vindictive. The accusations hurled at me today — I don't usually indulge in language but I think the word is appropriate — come in the course of duty. I brush them aside. But. We have to protect the innocent public.

GIRL. Right!

POLICEMAN. For their sake I demand the utmost severity. Thankyou.

JUDGE. Young man?

MAN. I didn't do it!

JUDGE. But offer no proof. (*Chinks the coins patiently*.)

Poem of Naivety

MAN (*recites*):
    When I left home my parents
    Gave me seven coins for the journey
    They said if the journey is long
    And these coins don't reach
    Look in your soul
    There you will find
    All that is needful

To thine ownself be true
The rest will follow

JUDGE (*leans forward and picks something from the* MAN). You
haven't got a soul. You can't carry a stone *and* a soul. A soul is
the heaviest thing in the world. When you took up the stone
your soul fell out of the bottom of your trousers. (*Cracks his
fingers.*) You have only a louse — which *is* an anagram of soul
if you add an E. But the E is silent! (*Formally.*) The sentence!
I am a philanthropic nature. You strayed from the narrow
way. It's not my intention to chase you off it altogether. I
shall guide you back to it — set your nose to the grindstone,
your feet on the path of duty to your master —

MAN. She said he was dead!

GIRL. Liar!

JUDGE. I order that the stone which you have carried till now
shall in future be chained to you —

MAN. No!

JUDGE. — and removed only at the mason's house. That will
certainly stop you straying far from the narrow way.

MAN. No!

POLICEMAN. When you're chained you won't have the strength
to argue.

The POLICEMAN *takes the* MAN *out.*

GIRL. I turn my back on life. I'll go in a nunnery.

JUDGE. Impossible. It's your duty to run your inn and dance for
the public.

GIRL. If that's the court's ruling.

JUDGE. But I'll have to raise the rent.

GIRL. Do what!

JUDGE. Double it. I must ensure that only a good class of person
can afford to get in. No more hooliganism.

GIRL. I can't pay anymore! We're screwing the customers now!

JUDGE. Think about it. And the alternative.

GIRL (*spits*). A fly in my mouth.

The JUDGE *and the* GIRL *leave.*

Scene Five

Road. Empty stage. The MAN *enters. He is old and broken. The stone is very big. It's chained to his back. He staggers forwards in sudden lurches.*

MAN. I came to a river. I stepped in the ferryboat. My stone was heavy. The boat sank. The ferryman beat me with his pole. I climbed far up in the mountain. I dragged the stone after me. Yes. Inch by inch. Year after year. At the top I came to the source of the river. The land was spread before me. In the distance a white cloud came up from the earth: steam or smoke. Then I knew: dust! The quarry! I started to hurry down. O the idiocy of it! The journey up was light, light, light to the journey down! The stone dragged me after it as if it was alive. The mountain was steep. I fought all the way. Year after year. At nights I propped it on a ledge and slept. An animal under its stone. Often it rolled away. I woke up. Dragged down in the dark by my chain. I cry at the stupidity of my life. Wasted on dragging a stone to somewhere I don't know for a reason I don't understand.

BOY *comes in.*

MAN. Help me put this down.

BOY. Who are you? (*Helps the* MAN *lower the stone to the ground.*) Why did they do this to you?

MAN. I'm looking for the mason's house.

BOY. You're almost there.

MAN. Almost — ? You know it? Where? Where?

BOY. Follow the road over the field. It's down in the lane on the other side.

MAN. His house is here? I've reached his house?

BOY (*points*). In five minutes.

MAN. The end . . . The end . . . Sometimes I thought I was lost. Taken the wrong road. I'd never get there. But after a few months I saw the cloud. Far in the distance. For an hour or more. Sometimes even at night in the full moon. I knew one day I'd be here, at the last steps . . .

BOY. Shall I help?

MAN. No — it's easy.

The BOY *goes out.*

MAN.

Help, or Song of Experience

You come smiling to offer service
You bring two good hands to help
Your face is open and guileless

But you find you are too weak to help
The grain you wanted to take to the farmers
Is in a tower — with guards at the door

You haven't even got the things that are yours
To get them you have to fight
The steps of your journey measure out a duel
And the weapons are chosen by your enemy

He goes.

Scene Six

Outside the MASON's *House. Empty stage. An old*
WASHERWOMAN *comes on with a washtub and washboard. She*
wears a floral apron. She washes white sheets.

The MAN *comes in.*

MAN. Is this the mason's house?

WOMAN. Yes.

MAN. Is the mason in?

WOMAN. He expecting you?

MAN. He told me to bring this stone.

WOMAN. Put it down.

MAN (*puts the stone down*). Call him.

WOMAN. He won't come out. You'll have to go in. (*Points to the*
stone.) And leave that there. He won't have any work in the
house. (*She takes a key from her apron pocket and throws it at*

him.) Catch.

MAN (*unfastens his chain*). There.

WOMAN. Now wash your face and hands. He won't have
any dirt in the house. Says there's enough muck in the yard.
The windows are always covered. Keeps the dust out.
Curtains never drawn. The yard's a muck hole. Dirt hangs in
the air. (*She brushes his coat. He washes in the tub*.) I do all
the washing. They get black working in the yard. And he —
(*Gestures to the house*.) — gets worse on the roads. (*Hands
him the towel*.) It's a lot of work.

MAN (*dries himself and hands the towel back*). Thank you.

WOMAN (*looks at him*). Much better. Something else he's fussy
about — I have to ask everyone — any money?

MAN. Yes.

WOMAN. Fetch it out.

MAN (*takes the seven coins*). That's all.

WOMAN. See? — covered in muck. Can't see what they are.
Greasy dirty things. In the tub. (*She washes the coins*.)

MAN. What's the machine in the yard? A huge concrete
rhinoceros with great steel paws.

WOMAN. Look, like new! (*Dries the coins*.) What have we got?
You're well off. (*Reads the coins:*) Prudence, soberness,
courage, justice, love — (*Drops a coin*.) Butterfingers. (*Fishes
it out*.) Hope. Mint condition! Well the mason will be glad. I
expect he'll ask you to stay. In you go. Can't stop and chatter.
Work to do. All this to hang up yet. And wipe your feet.

The WOMAN *goes out with the tub and board. The* MAN *waits
till she's gone. He fastens the chain round him as if it was
locked. He picks up the stone and goes.*

Scene Seven

The MASON's *House. It is dark. The* MASON *is much older. He
kneels by a bucket and a small heap of stones.*

MASON (*mumbling to himself*). Dirt on the tables. In the clocks.

Damn woman cheats. I shut the doors. Block up the
keyholes —

A knock.

MASON. Come. Quickly.

The MAN *comes in. He carries the stone.*

MASON. Take that out! I won't have that in here! Out! (*Calls.*)
Woman! (*To* MAN:) Who are you! What d'you — ?

MAN. You told me to come.

MASON. Take that out!

MAN. Long ago.

MASON. Long ago?

MAN. You gave me a stone. I had seven coins.

MASON (*yells*). Woman! (*To* MAN:) Seven coins? Gold. Yes,
perhaps. Long ago. You were a boy. (*Calls.*) Woman! (*To*
MAN:) You've taken your time.

MAN. The stone was heavy.

MASON. But you brought it. I remember now. Good family
background. Thrifty people. They gave you the right start.
Well — have you still got it?

MAN. Yes.

MASON. Washed?

MAN. Yes.

MASON. Show me, show me.

The MAN *takes out the seven gold coins.*

MASON. Yes, sparkling! Gold. New after all these years!
Prudence, soberness, courage, justice, honesty, love — and
what was the other one? Hope. Now you shall be rewarded.
I'll make you a servant in my house.

MAN. Why did the coins change?

MASON. But I don't know why she didn't unfasten your stone.
She's got the key. Silly woman!

MAN. Why did the stone grow?

MASON (*blandly*). We get older. We carry the weight of the
world on our shoulders. We make heavy weather. (*He picks up*

a stone from the pile, holds it over the bucket, squeezes, and the blood trickles down. Calls:) Woman!

MAN. Why did the coins change?

MASON. Change?

MAN. From justice to anger, from hope to pride?

MASON. They didn't change.

MAN. From temperance to greed, from love to envy?

MASON. You got confused. Easiest thing. I told you — they make heavy weather.

MAN. They changed.

MASON. You couldn't tell what they were. Under that dirt? Look at them now. Prudence, soberness. Look! Justice, honesty —

MAN. They changed.

MASON (*takes a stone and starts to squeeze it. Blood drips*). Servants don't argue. (*Stops squeezing.*) I remember you were a bit difficult.

MAN. I tell you they changed.

MASON. You say that like an idiot! (*Squeezes again. More blood.*) I'm afraid I can't let you work in my house after all. You'll have to work in the yard.

MAN. Why was the stone so heavy?

MASON. I see you're a trouble maker. No wonder she didn't unchain you. She knew what she was doing. (*Calls:*) Woman!

MAN. Why did I waste my life carrying your load?

MASON (*squeezing stones*). You've ruined your only chance. I wash my hands of you. You're just more dirt that's got in through the door. You've lived with dirt so long you're as full of it as the worm under its stone. Fool, arguing! I can get blood out of a stone — and you stand there questioning me?

MAN. Why did the stone grow?

MASON. A servant bringing dirt in my house. My house is a palace. Making me shout when I reverence silence. What? Why? Who? In my yard there's a machine. You saw it? Huge. With a beak. People bring their stones to my yard all day. The machine crushes them down to *this* — heart-size to fit in the hand. But it can't get the blood. They're passed to me. The master-craftsman. And so —. (*He squeezes a stone. It trickles.*) What else? What's at the end of the road? The hole in the road. Why does it take so long? You march till you die! Why are you chained? Because I don't trust you! —

The MAN *leaves the stone and comes to the* MASON.

MAN. Look! Envy — greed — !

MASON. What — ! (*Calls:*) Woman! Foreman!

The MAN *grabs the* MASON *and shows him the coins.*

MAN. Sloth — gluttony —

MASON. Help! Help!

MAN (*holds the coins in front of the* MASON's *face*). Look! Look! Lust!

MASON. No!

MAN. Pride! Anger! (*Drops the coins.*) And now I shall kill you.

MASON. You won't. No. There's no reason. (*Calls:*) Help! Talk. Discuss. You're right. You must be. If it means so much. Tell me. Go to the window. Look. I'm rich. (*Calmer.*) Yes how natural. You envy my quarry, my yard. (*Still more calm.*) I'll make you a partner. It's time I had new blood — (*Quickly.*) new — the enterprise needs new management. You're our sort. (*Wheedling.*) I applaud all this. Initiative. It's time for a change. The new men are —

The MAN *kills the* MASON *by crushing him with the stone. He stares at the body for a moment. He looks up.*

MAN (*calls calmly*): Woman! Call the men to break the machine in the yard.

WOMAN (*off*). Do you want water to wash your hands?

MAN (*calls calmly*): No need. They are clean.